14+

BREAK THROUGH

to CLIL

for

Biology

T0344213

Matthew Broderick
Timothy Chadwick

CAMBRIDGE
UNIVERSITY PRESS

CAMBRIDGE
UNIVERSITY PRESS

University Printing House, Cambridge CB2 8BS, United Kingdom

One Liberty Plaza, 20th Floor, New York, NY 10006, USA

477 Williamstown Road, Port Melbourne, VIC 3207, Australia

4843/24, 2nd Floor, Ansari Road, Daryaganj, Delhi – 110002, India

79 Anson Road, #06–04/06, Singapore 079906

Cambridge University Press is part of the University of Cambridge.

It furthers the University's mission by disseminating knowledge in the pursuit of
education, learning and research at the highest international levels of excellence.

www.cambridge.org
Information on this title: education.cambridge.org

© Cambridge University Press 2015

First published 2015
20 19 18 17 16 15 14 13 12 11 10 9 8 7

Printed in Great Britain by CPI Group (UK) Ltd, Croydon CR0 4YY

A catalogue record for this publication is available from the British Library

ISBN 978-1-107-69983-0 Paperback

Contents

Introduction

Note to students

Welcome to this workbook, which will help you with your study of biology using English. To progress well in your studies in biology, it will help if you can also use the English language well in a way that is appropriate to science. If you can read English well, you can understand what is written in your biology textbook easily. If you can write and speak English well, you can share your knowledge about biology with others easily.

This workbook will help you understand some important topics in biology. It will also help you develop your skills in English. The exercises will give you practice in both things at the same time.

The exercises will help your English skills in different ways. They will:

- help you understand the meaning of important words
- help you to use certain types of words correctly, like nouns and adjectives
- help you to construct sentences correctly
- help you to construct whole passages of text
- give you practice in reading text and extracting information from it.

Each unit in this book covers a different area of biology, but almost exclusively covers the Core IGCSE topics. You do not need to complete all the units in the order in which they appear in the book. Instead, as you are being taught a certain area of biology in the classroom, you should complete the exercises in the unit that covers that area. Your teacher may ask you to work on the exercises at home or in class.

Throughout the text you will see language boxes like this one. These boxes give you some background information about the English language skills that you are learning about. If you see the icon ![icon], this means you can read more about that area of English language in the *Language file* at the back of this book.

> A *rule* is the same as a *ruler*. It is a special term used for a ruler that is one metre long.

You will also find an *Answer key* for the exercises at the back of this book. You can use this to check whether your answers are correct. Sometimes there are many different possible answers to a question. The *Answer key* will make it clear that the suggested answer is just an example, and your own answer might look different. In these cases, look carefully at the structure of your answer, to see if it is the same as the answer in the *Answer key*. There are notes in the *Answer key* that will help you to see if your answer is a correct one. If you are still not sure, then ask your teacher to help you.

We hope you enjoy using this book, and that you progress well in your studies of biology and English.

The Breakthrough to CLIL team

Note to teachers

This book is designed to help EAL/ESL/E2L students understand the content of their biology course and build English language skills within the context of their biology studies, though you may also use it to support students who have English as their first language. It is intended for use within the context of a biology course, rather than an English course, but almost exclusively covers the Core IGCSE topics. If your school has an embedded CLIL or bilingual programme, you may find this book suitable to support most or all of your students in their studies. However, this book can also be used as part of your differentiation for a smaller number of students who would benefit from it, whether in the classroom or as homework.

The areas of biology covered in this book are the basic topics that most students aged around 14 to 16 would encounter. However, most students would also be expected to be familiar with some other topics, as well as covering the topics included in this book in more detail. The intention of this book is to help students master the basics, and develop language skills and confidence that will help them in other parts of their course. This book should be used to support a wider learning programme that also includes a textbook of an appropriate level.

The areas of English language covered in this book have been selected for their relevance to understanding and discussing the subject of biology. Where aspects of language are discussed explicitly, this is intended to help students understand the purpose of certain exercises, as well as explain why these aspects of language are relevant to biology. It is expected that the students will be able to link these explanations to the content of their English language (or E2L) course. We hope that you as a biology teacher will feel confident enough in the areas of language discussed to support your students, with the help of the explanations provided in the text and the *Language file*. If not, we advise you to discuss the content of this book with a colleague in your English department.

Each unit of this book covers a certain area of biology. Within each unit, the level of demand in terms of both biology and English gradually increases. This will allow students to build understanding and language skills as they progress through each unit. The first exercise in each unit does require some familiarity with key vocabulary and concepts, so we recommend that you begin to set the exercises in this book after having taught a lesson or two on the relevant topic. The units have been designed to be used independently from one another, so you can set them in any order to match your existing teaching programme.

We hope that you will enjoy using this book with your students.

The Breakthrough to CLIL team

1 Classification

This unit covers:

- ☐ the seven characteristics of living organisms
- ☐ using the binomial system of naming species

Exercise 1.1 Characteristics of living organisms

All living things share seven characteristics. Anything that does not have all seven characteristics is not alive. This exercise will help you recognise the words for the seven characteristics, and what each one means.

1   The names of the seven characteristics for living things are hidden in this wordsnake. The scientific term for a living thing is also in the wordsnake.

Draw lines between the words to separate them.

2   Now write each word you found after the correct definition.

   a   A living thing. ....

   b   The removal of waste products and other unwanted substances. ....

   c   The increase in size and dry mass of an organism. ....

   d   The changing of position or place by an organism. ....

   e   The consumption of nutrients in order to provide the raw materials for growth.

   ....

   f   The production of offspring. ....

   g   The release of energy from nutrient molecules. ....

   h   The ability to detect and respond to a change in the environment. ....

Exercise 1.2 Unusual plurals

> This exercise will help you recognise some unusual plural forms used in this area of biology.

If you read through any biology textbook, you will see that there are many words that can be written in **singular** or **plural** form. You use the singular form if you are talking about just one of something, and the plural if you are talking about more than one.

Often the plural form is just the singular form with the ending -*s*, for example:

   Singular: Hair is a *characteristic* of all mammals.

   Plural: Living organisms share seven *characteristics*.

Sometimes, the plural form is not so simple, it is *irregular.* For example:

   Singular: A *bacterium* is a very primitive type of organism.

   Plural: The *bacteria* belong to the kingdom of the prokaryotes.

It is important for you to be able to recognise and use irregular plurals.

Below, some irregular plural forms from this unit have been scrambled. Unscramble each example and insert it in the gap in the sentence provided. Then write down the singular form of the word.

Here is an example to help you:

> HLYPA
>
> The five phyla in the animal kingdom are: mammals, birds, fish, reptiles and amphibians.
>
> Singular: phylum

1 RENGAE

The names of .... always begin with a capital letter.

Singular: ....

2 IFNUG

Mushrooms and yeast are examples of ....

Singular: ....

3 PECSISE

Members of two different .... usually cannot breed with each other.

Singular: ....

Exercise 1.3 Constructing a key – writing opposites

> This is an important exercise that will enable you to form sentences when constructing a key.

If you don't know the name of an organism, or what group it belongs to, you can use a *key*. A key consists of pairs of definitions. When you choose the definition that matches your organism, you are led to the next choice. In the end, you get the name of your organism or the group it belongs to.

Writing keys is an important skill for biologists. You are expected to write sentences that mean *opposites* to allow the reader of the key to clearly identify whether a particular characteristic is present or not. For example:

> The organism *has* eight legs.
>
> The organism *does not have* eight legs.

The reader of the key can easily decide whether the organism has eight legs or not before moving on to the next option.

A key has been constructed below to help classify these organisms into their classes:

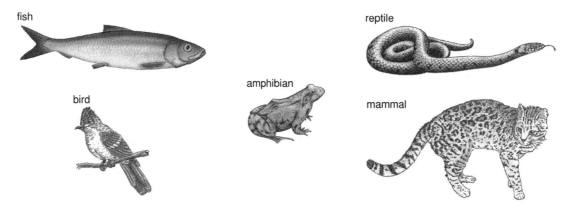

fish

reptile

bird

amphibian

mammal

Complete the missing definitions to allow the reader to follow the key. The first example has been done for you.

Use the diagrams above to help you identify the missing classes.

I	The organism is homeothermic (warm-blooded).	Go to II
	The organism is not homeothermic.	Go to III
II	The organism feeds its young on milk.	1 ....
	2	BIRD
III	3	AMPHIBIAN
	The organism does not have a moist, smooth skin.	Go to IV
IV	The organism has gills and fins.	4 ....
	5	REPTILE

Exercise 1.4 Describing organisms

> In this exercise you will learn about the characteristics of mammals. You will also practise the skill of extracting information from a text.

The different features of an organism help us to classify each of them into different groups. These features are the *characteristics* that allow us to do this.

For example, an animal with wings and feathers can be placed in the class 'birds', as it is easy to observe these features. There will be other characteristics that we can't see.

Read the text below, then answer the questions.

> Human beings (*Homo sapiens*) belong to the class Mammalia (mammals). Mammals can be recognised by visible characteristics, such as the presence of fur or hair. They feed their young from their mammary glands. If you look closely enough, you will see that mammals have different types of teeth, such as incisors and canines. We know that mammals have a placenta and a diaphragm, and that a mammalian heart has four chambers. Mammals have well-developed brains. They are able to adapt and survive in a wide range of different conditions. Mammals, like birds, are homeothermic and have to maintain a constant internal body temperature. Some mammals, such as cats, have whiskers that are sensitive to touch and vibrations.

1   Which genus do human beings belong to? ....

2   List **four** of the *observable* characteristics of mammals mentioned in the text.

....

....

3   List **four** characteristics of mammals we know are true but can't see when watching them in the wild. (Use your dictionary if some of these terms are new.)

....

....

4   Which word from the text shows that mammals are warm-blooded? ....

5   How do you think a 'well-developed brain' enables mammals to adapt and survive?

....

....

6   How do you think incisors and canines help a mammal such as a lion to survive?

....

....

Exercise 1.5 Using prefixes to define words

This exercise will help you to use prefixes to determine what a word means. This will be useful to you in this unit, as well as in other areas of biology.

A lot of scientific terms are a combination of some of these parts: a **prefix**, a **root** and a **suffix**.

If we take a word from medicine like *hypoglycemia*, it looks like a difficult term. However, if we know the three parts of the term, we can understand the meaning. 'Glyco', the root, is sugar, 'emia', the suffix, is blood, and 'hypo', the prefix, means low or below. And so hypoglycemia means low blood sugar.

In the following exercise we will focus on common prefixes from biology. If you know the meaning of the prefix – the first part of a scientific term – this can help you understand what the whole word means and help you remember them in a logical way.

If we take *photosynthesis*, the prefix 'photo' means light. The word 'synthesis' means to combine things to form something new.

Photosynthesis is the process by which plants use light to make their own food.

Read the sentences below. Identify the prefixes in the words written in italics. Write down what you think each prefix means.

Here is an example to help you.

Bacteria are an example of *unicellular* organisms.

Prefix: uni-

Prefix meaning: one

1   I can use a *dichotomous* key to identify an organism.

Prefix: ....

Prefix meaning: ....

2   Arthropods are *invertebrates* that have an *exoskeleton*.

Prefix 1: ....   Prefix 2: ....

Prefix 1 meaning: ....   Prefix 2 meaning: ....

3 *Monocotyledonous* plants are usually known as monocots.

Prefix: ....

Prefix meaning: ....

4 A plant cell contains many *chloroplasts* to absorb light energy.

Prefix: ....

Prefix meaning: ....

Exercise 1.6 Kingdom to species – using the key words in context

It is sometimes easy to recall the different levels of organisation from kingdom to species. It is much more challenging to use these words in your own writing. This exercise will help you to remember the order of the classification groups and give you practice at using the terms in a report.

1 Below is a description of an organism. Complete the text using the terms below:

backbone	binomial	*Bos*	family	kingdom
Mammalia	order	phylum	plants	species

A cow is commonly known as 'cattle' and is a member of the .... *Bos primigenius*. From this .... name we can say that the cow must be grouped in the genus ....

Like many members of the Bovidae .... , the cow is herbivorous and only eats ....

The next group that the cow belongs to is Artiodactyla – this is the .... , and includes many other similar families.

The cow belongs to the class .... because it has hair, suckles its young and is homeothermic (maintains a constant internal body temperature).

This animal has a .... , which places them in the .... Chordata.

Finally, the cow is an important member of the Animalia ....

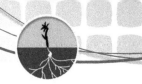

2   Now it is your turn to produce a description of an organism. You can use the text about the cow above to help you. Choose an organism that interests you and research the information you need in books or on the internet.

Include the following information in your description:

■   The names of each group that your organism fits into. For example, the lion belongs to the family *Felidae*.

■   At least three observable characteristics of your chosen organism that explain why it belongs to a particular group, and three that we can't observe while the organism is alive.

Use the space below to complete your answer:

....

....

....

....

....

....

....

....

....

....

....

....

....

....

2 Cell structure and function

This unit covers:

- ☐ the differences between animal and plant cells
- ☐ how the structure of a cell relates to its function
- ☐ the arrangement of cells, tissues, organs and organ systems
- ☐ how the random movement of molecules contributes to diffusion and osmosis

Exercise 2.1 The parts of a cell

In this exercise you will look at the different parts of a cell. You are expected to be able to describe the general function of these parts within a cell.

1 Some parts of cells are labelled in these diagrams. Write the name of each part next to the correct definition below.

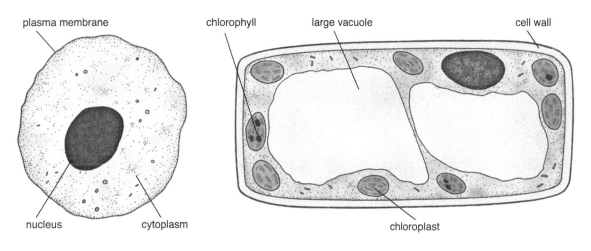

a This contains chlorophyll for photosynthesis. ....

b This is a space within a cell that contains a solution. ....

c Substances are able to pass in and out of the cell through this. ....

d Made of cellulose and provides strength to the cell. ....

e The jelly-like substance that fills the cell. ....

f Stores genetic information. ....

g Absorbs sunlight for photosynthesis. ....

2 Some of the structures in question **1** are only found in plant cells, and some are found in both plant and animal cells. Write the names of the seven structures discussed in question **1** in the correct column of the table below. Two examples have been done for you.

Plant cell only	Plant cell and animal cell
large vacuole	plasma membrane

Exercise 2.2 Comparing cells

Test and examination questions often require you to compare the structure of different cells. In this exercise you will practise the correct language to use when making comparisons.

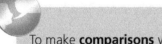

To make **comparisons** you use phrases like:

Cell A has *more* mitochondria than cell B.

Cell A *has* a tail, but cell B *does not*.

The above sentences describe *differences* between two cells.

The two cells *both* contain a cell wall.

This sentence describes a *similarity* between two cells.

It is important that you mention both cells in your answer.

Look at the diagrams below. Complete the comparative sentences to describe similarities or differences between the cells.

Here is an example to help you.

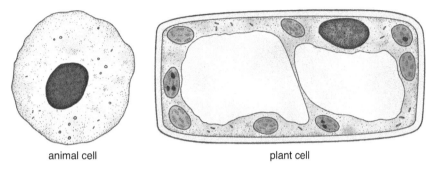

animal cell   plant cell

The plant cell has a cell wall, but the animal cell does not.

1

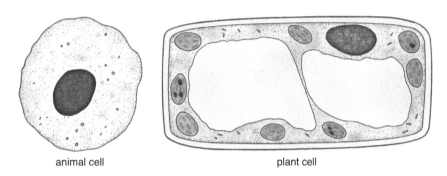

animal cell   plant cell

The plant cell and the animal cell .... a nucleus.

2

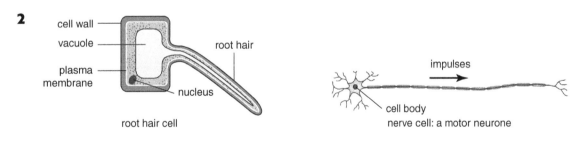

cell wall
vacuole
plasma membrane
nucleus
root hair
root hair cell

impulses
cell body
nerve cell: a motor neurone

The root hair cell has a large vacuole, but ....

....

3

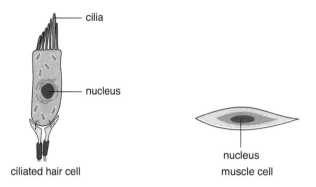

ciliated hair cell

nucleus
muscle cell

The ciliated hair cell has small hairs to trap mucus, but ....

....

4

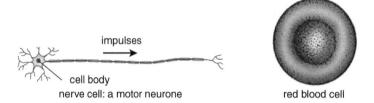

nerve cell: a motor neurone

red blood cell

The red blood cell does not contain a nucleus, but ....

....

5 Now write a complete sentence of your own comparing animal and plant cells.

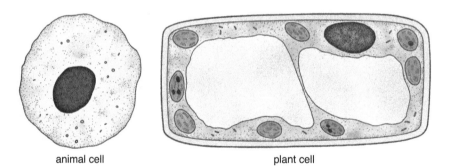

animal cell

plant cell

....

....

Exercise 2.3 Organisation of cells

> This exercise will help you to describe a specific cell, tissue, organ or organ system with real examples from different organisms. You should be able to describe examples of these at any level within an organism.

There are many different types of specialised *cell* in an organism. Cells that have a similar structure and function work together as a *tissue*. Several tissues may then combine to form *organs*. Organs work together in *organ systems*. A collection of organ systems forms an *organism*.

Choose the correct term to complete the following sentences. Cross out the incorrect term(s).

Here is an example to help you:

> A leaf is an example of ~~a tissue~~/an organ found in many types of plant.

> Remember that we usually use *an* when the next word, a noun, begins with a vowel (a, e, i, o or u).

1   The eye is a type of cell/tissue/organ found in many animals.

2   A thin layer of cells/tissues called the epithelium provides protection for various parts of the body.

3   The oesophagus, stomach, liver and pancreas are all cells/tissues/organs found within a typical digestive system/body.

4   A root hair cell/tissue absorbs water and minerals for plants to use.

5   The trachea contains ciliated cells/tissues that work to trap and remove mucus from the body.

6   Nerve impulses are sent around the body by nerve cells/tissue.

7   Blood is a tissue/an organ that contains red blood cells/tissues and transports substances around the body.

8   Muscle cells work together in muscle tissue/organs to allow the heart to contract and pump blood around the body.

9   The small intestine is a collection of tissues that work together as an organ system/organ to digest food substances.

Exercise 2.4 Describing diffusion

> When you are learning about diffusion, it is important that you are able to use this knowledge to describe what happens to the particles in any given situation. It is also important that you use the correct scientific language.

Diffusion is the movement of molecules from a high concentration to a low concentration. Diffusion is one way in which particles can move in and out of cells across the partially permeable cell membrane.

The diagrams in the questions show different situations where diffusion may take place. You will be asked to write sentences that describe what will happen to the particles labelled. The following key words are available for you to use.

concentration gradient   **diffuse**   **high concentration**

low concentration   **(oxygen) molecules**   **partially permeable membrane**

Here is an example to help you.

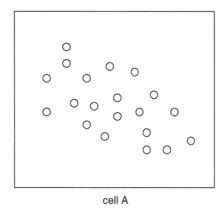
cell A

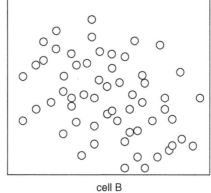
cell B

Model answer:

> The *molecules* in cell B will *diffuse* down the *concentration gradient* to cell A.

Or:

> The *molecules* will move from a *high concentration* in cell B to a *lower concentration* in cell A.

1   Look at the diagram, then complete the sentences below. Cross out the incorrect words where you have a choice.

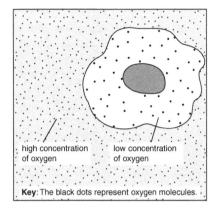

high concentration of oxygen

low concentration of oxygen

Key: The black dots represent oxygen molecules.

The concentration of oxygen molecules is higher/lower outside the cell than inside. This will cause the molecules of oxygen to move into/out of the cell. The oxygen molecules will diffuse/transport across the membrane. The membrane of the cell is partially/fully permeable to allow diffusion to take place.

2   Now look at this diagram. Write a short paragraph below to describe what will happen to the oxygen molecules this time. Use the key words and model answers given above to help you.

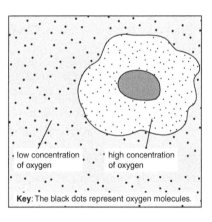

low concentration of oxygen

high concentration of oxygen

Key: The black dots represent oxygen molecules.

....

....

....

....

Exercise 2.5 Describing and explaining osmosis

> This exercise focuses on the difference between the terms *describe* and *explain*. You will also improve your understanding of osmosis experiments, and your ability to use a graph.

In science questions, you will be given **command words**. These are verbs that tell you what to do in the question.

Describe and *explain* are common examples of command words.

If you are asked to *describe* a graph, it means you should write what you see. Do not *explain* the data. For example:

Chung's breathing rate increased rapidly after 3 minutes.

If you are asked to *explain* what you see in a graph, you must give the scientific reasons how or why something has happened. For example:

Chung's breathing rate increased because his muscles were using up oxygen for respiration and he needed to take more oxygen into his body.

The following paragraph describes and explains osmosis. Don't forget that the vocabulary in Exercise 2.1 can help you here:

Osmosis is the movement of water molecules through a partially permeable membrane down a concentration gradient. Cell membranes are partially permeable, so osmosis can occur through them. If a cell is placed in a solution that is *more* concentrated than the cytoplasm, water will move *out of* the cell. If a cell is placed in a solution that is *less* concentrated than the cytoplasm, water will move *into* the cell.

Shilpa performed an experiment to study osmosis. She placed a piece of potato in a concentrated sugar solution. She measured the mass of the potato every minute.

The diagrams show what Shilpa observed.

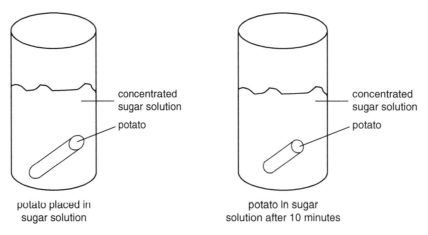

potato placed in
sugar solution

potato in sugar
solution after 10 minutes

Shilpa drew this graph to present her results:

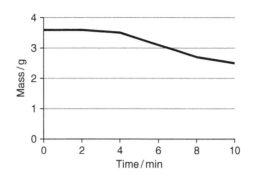

time / min	mass / g
0	3.6
2	3.6
4	3.5
6	3.1
8	2.7
10	2.5

1 Describe what Shilpa's graph shows. Look at the graph and observe what happens to the mass of the potato. At what time does the mass of the potato start changing?

In general, the graph shows the change in ....

....

Specifically, it can be observed that after .... minutes, ...

....

....

2 Explain what Shilpa's graph shows. Why has the mass of the potato changed? Use your knowledge of osmosis to explain this change.

The mass of the potato changed because ....

....

....

....

....

3 The chemicals of life

This unit covers:

☐ the different chemicals that allow our bodies to function
☐ how to test for the presence of some chemicals
☐ what an enzyme is and how it functions within the body
☐ the names and uses of different enzymes

Exercise 3.1 Chemicals of life – vocabulary

This exercise will help you to understand some of the key terms that appear throughout this unit. It is useful for you to understand these key words and how they contribute to a healthy organism.

Some of the words are also used in chemistry.

Below is a list of definitions. The spaces between the words have been removed. Draw lines between the words to divide the sentences again. Then, find a key word from this list that fits the definition.

atom   carbohydrate   element   metabolism   molecule   water

Here is an example to help you:

A/protein/that/acts/as/a/biological/catalyst.   enzyme

1 Asubstancethatcannotbebrokendownintoanythingsimpler.   ....

2 Asingleparticleofanelement.   ....

3 Twoormoreatomsjoinedtogether.   ....

4 Chemicalreactionsthattakeplaceinthebody.   ....

5 Ausefulsubstancethatmakesup80%ofthebody.   ....

6 Moleculethatcontainscarbonhydrogenandoxygen.   ....

Exercise 3.2 Sentences about carbohydrates

In this exercise you will practise what you know about carbohydrates. You will also develop your understanding of prefixes.

Carbohydrates are a class of substances that includes starches, sugars and cellulose. They all contain carbon, hydrogen and oxygen atoms.

The different types of carbohydrates can be classified into groups depending on their structure. The clue to this is in their name.

The **prefix** of many scientific terms will help you understand or remember what the term means. In this case they refer to numbers. For example:

*Mono*cotyledon refers to seeds that have *one* cotyledon only.

The *tri*cuspid valve in the heart has *three* points.

The different sugars in the carbohydrate group can be described as simple or complex sugars. A simple or complex sugar will have a name that will help you to see this.

1 **a** Complete the table below to show that you understand the different prefixes for carbohydrates and examples of them. Use the words below.

| di- | glucose | maltose | monosaccharide | one |
| poly- | two | polysaccharide | starch | many |

Prefix/meaning	Type of sugar	Example
mono-/one	....	....
.... /	disaccharide	sucrose and ....
.... /	....	cellulose and ....

b Use two of the words again to complete the definition.

.... such as cellulose are made up of .... units of sugar and resemble a long chain. This is why they are known as complex sugars.

2 Glucose is a carbohydrate that is vital to the chemical process of respiration. Respiration is the process that will release the stored energy in glucose to allow an organism to grow and be healthy.

Complete these sentences about this important simple sugar by crossing out the incorrect terms.

Glucose is a simple/complex sugar that is made up of six cobalt/carbon atoms joined together in a ring. Six/Twelve hydrogen atoms are attached to the carbon atoms, as well as six oxygen/hydrogen atoms.

3 You are going to read about an experiment. First you need to know something about the carbohydrate glucose. Unscramble the words to make a simple definition of glucose.

Glucose ($C_6H_{12}O_6$) is a *plisme edirahccaonosm* found in *lanspt*. It is absorbed directly into our *doolb* during digestion and is a vital source of *reneyg*.

.........simple.................

....

....

....

....

Exercise 3.3 Planning a food test

This exercise is about testing foods to see if they contain certain chemicals. You will also learn about using the imperative form in instructions, and using the passive form when describing what you did in an experiment.

Barikis has planned an experiment that will allow her to test for the presence of glucose in a sample of food.

1 a Barikis has written some instructions about how to test for the presence of glucose in a sample of food. However, the instructions are in the *wrong* order. Put the instructions in the correct order, numbering them from 1 to 8. The first has been done for you.

A Cut the food up into very small pieces. ....

B Add Benedict's solution to the test tube. ....

C Dissolve the food in water in a test tube. ....

D Record the results in the results chart. ....

E Collect the necessary equipment, including your safety spectacles. ....1...................

F   Draw a results chart. ....

G   Observe whether the solution turns orange-red showing glucose is present.

    ....

H   Strongly <u>heat</u> the test tube in a water bath. ....

b   Read the information about instructions. Then, underline the imperatives in Exercise 1a. An example has been done for you from sentence H.

Barikis's instructions are written in the **imperative**. In imperatives we use the basic form of the verb to tell someone what to do. When Barikis writes her report, she needs to write what she did. She will describe the same actions, but in a different form. An appropriate form is the **passive**. Scientists often use the passive voice because *what is happening* is more important than who is performing the action. There are three simple steps for turning an instruction into a passive sentence.

Here is an instruction: *Record the volume of water.*

To make this instruction passive:

1   Find the object of the sentence. The object is the 'thing' that the verb is acting on: *the volume of water.* This becomes the subject of the new sentence.

2   Choose between *was* or *were*. You use *was* if the object is singular and *were* if it is plural. So in this case: *was.*

3   Next, use the **past participle** of the verb. When you see three forms of a verb given – such as *take/took/taken* – the past participle is the third form. The past participle of *to record* is: *recorded.*

This gives you the passive sentence:

   The volume of water was recorded.

2   Rewrite Barikis's instructions in the correct order so that they are in the passive. The first one has been done for you.

    The necessary equipment was collected, including our safety spectacles.

a   The food ....

b   ....

c   ....

d   ....

e ....

f ....

g ....

3 The series of diagrams below shows you how to carry out simple food tests. Use the diagrams to answer the questions that follow.

a

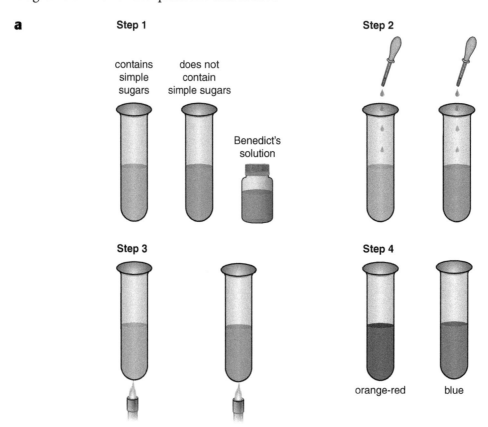

Complete the following sentences about the four stages of the food test. The sentences require more input from you as they progress.

i Step 1 shows a test tube containing a solution of simple sugars. ....
... is an example of a simple sugar.

ii Step 2 shows .... being added to the
....

iii Step 3 shows the test tubes ....

iv Step 4 shows ....
....

v The solution in the test tube that contains simple sugars has turned from
.... to ....

b

Step 1

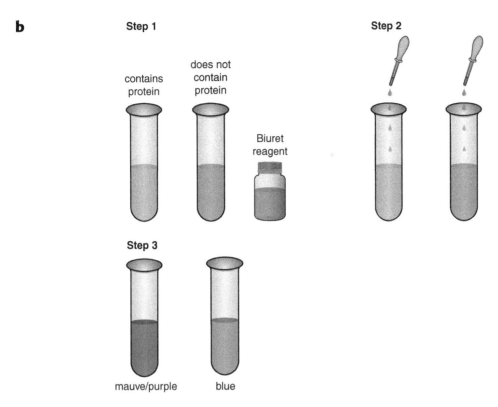

contains protein

does not contain protein

Biuret reagent

Step 2

Step 3

mauve/purple   blue

This time, you should write a full sentence of your own to describe what is happening at each step of the food test.

i   Step 1 shows ....

....

ii   Step 2 shows ....

....

iii   Step 3 shows ....

....

iv   Food test **b** shows that the presence of .... will turn

.... reagent from .... to ....

Exercise 3.4 Key words for enzymes

> This exercise will help to develop your understanding of enzymes. It will also help you avoid some common mistakes students make when describing this topic.

The biology of enzymes is filled with many specialised key words. Understanding these key words will allow you to answer many questions related to enzymes and how they function. *Enzymes* make reactions happen faster when they combine with a *substrate* to produce *products*. These *reactions* happen more often at the correct *temperature* and *pH* (acidity) levels.

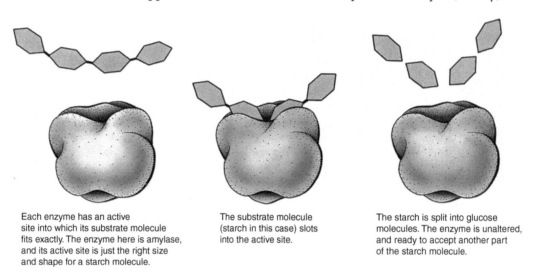

Each enzyme has an active site into which its substrate molecule fits exactly. The enzyme here is amylase, and its active site is just the right size and shape for a starch molecule.

The substrate molecule (starch in this case) slots into the active site.

The starch is split into glucose molecules. The enzyme is unaltered, and ready to accept another part of the starch molecule.

If the temperature or pH is too low or too high, the enzyme will not work as well as it could do.

Selecting the correct word is a vital skill to allow you to explain what is happening during the use of enzymes. For example:

> The enzyme *denatured* as the temperature *increased*.

1 Complete the passage below with the correct key words about enzymes. You may need your dictionary:

> Enzymes are proteins that are biological catalysts/catalases. This means that enzymes can faster/speed up a chemical reaction. An enzyme will only work with a particular nutrient/substrate – they are complementary/complimentary to each other. Once the reaction has taken place at the passive/active site of the enzyme, a product/produce is released. The enzyme remains unchanged and continues catalyst/catalysing reactions. Enzymes work best at certain conditions of pH and heat/temperature. The ideal pH is known as the optimum/prime pH, and the ideal temperature is known as the optimum temperature. If the temperature or pH is too high, the enzyme will lose its shape and is said to be destroyed/denatured.

Exercise 3.5 Effect of temperature on enzymes

This exercise is about how enzymes work better at some temperatures than others. You will practise interpreting information from a graph.

The effect of pH and temperature on enzymes is often demonstrated in a graph.

You are expected to be able to observe what is happening in a graph and draw sensible conclusions from this that are linked to your scientific knowledge.

When describing what happens in a graph, you should try to include as much information as possible. Look at these examples:

  A   The rate of reaction went up.

  B   The rate of reaction increased as the temperature increased.

Notice how answer B uses the word increased and compares the rate of reaction to the temperature.

  C   The enzyme denatured at 38 °C.

  D   The enzyme stopped working at about 40 °C.

In this example, answer C uses the word denatured and the exact temperature. This is much better and more accurate than answer D.

The graph below shows how temperature affects the rate of reaction of an enzyme.

Remember that 'effect' is almost always used as a noun and 'affect' as a verb – try not to confuse them.

From the example above:

> 'The effect of pH and temperature on enzymes is often demonstrated in a graph.' This can also be written 'How pH and temperature affect enzymes is often demonstrated in a graph.'

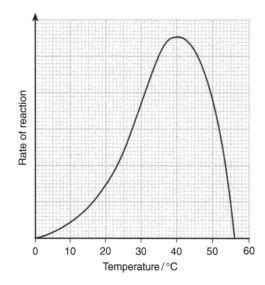

Use the graph to write a sentence that includes the following key words or phrases. Your sentence should include any data where necessary.

Here is an example to help you:

'rate of reaction is increasing'   The rate of reaction is increasing from 0°C to 40°C.

1   'optimum temperature'

    ....

    ....

2   'begins to denature'

    ....

    ....

3   'is completely denatured'

    ....

    ....

4   'the rate of reaction decreases because'

    ....

    ....

    ....

5 'the molecules have more kinetic energy'

....

....

....

Exercise 3.6 Using enzymes in industry

In this exercise you will learn about how enzymes are used in industry. You will practise the skill of extracting information from a section of text.

Enzymes are used in industry because the optimum conditions of the enzymes can be easily achieved. This allows companies to make their products work faster and better, which is good for those of us who use them.

Read the following text.

> Enzymes are biological catalysts that work best in their optimum conditions of pressure, temperature and pH. Enzymes are used commercially in many different ways.
>
> Pharmaceutical companies use catalase to speed up the healing of wounds. Catalase converts hydrogen peroxide to oxygen and water.
>
> Clothing, such as leather, is softened by using a specific protease. Stains can also be removed by enzymes: fats can be removed from clothing by adding lipases to washing powders. The fats are broken down into fatty acids and glycerol. This same method can be applied to use proteases to break down and remove proteins from clothing.
>
> Isomerase converts glucose to fructose to add a sweeter taste to some foods. Pectinase can be used to extract fruit juices for human consumption. Even babies can benefit from enzymes as proteases are added to formula milk to make digestion easier.

Answer the following questions based on the passage above.

1 Write down the name of the five enzymes that are mentioned in the text.

....

....

2 a What is the substrate that pharmaceutical companies target with catalase?

....

b What is this substrate broken down into?

....

3 What are lipids broken down into by lipase?

....

4 How might lipase and protease be denatured when washing clothes?

....

....

....

....

4 Animal nutrition

This unit covers:

☐ what makes up a balanced diet
☐ the role of different nutrients in our bodies
☐ the role of the alimentary canal in digestion
☐ how enzymes contribute to digestion

Exercise 4.1 Food versus nutrients

In this exercise you will distinguish clearly between what is *food* and what is a *nutrient*.

A *food* is a substance that can be eaten (ingested) in order to gain nutritional value from what is contained inside it.

A *nutrient* is a specific compound that can be found in the food that we eat. Nutrients allow us to grow and survive.

1 There are different foods and nutrients listed below.

Circle all of the foods in pen, and the seven different nutrients in pencil.

pasta	potato	egg	vitamins	orange	minerals	
cheese	bread	carbohydrates		butter	rice	
proteins	chicken	water	fats	fish	tomato	
ice cream	sugars	carrots	fibre	cheese	yoghurt	fries

2 Complete the sentences using the seven nutrients above.

a Pasta is a good source of ....

b Oranges and carrots are a good source of ...., ...

and ....

c Eggs, meat and fish are excellent foods for providing ....

d Ice cream contains a lot of .... and ....

e Bottled or tap .... satisfies our need for ....

Exercise 4.2 Using the correct word to suggest a more balanced diet

In this exercise you will practise the language you should use to give people advice on their diet.

We have seen the seven nutrient groups that we need. A *balanced diet* is when all of these nutrient groups are consumed in the correct amounts and proportions. This will allow the body to grow and develop in a healthy manner.

Sometimes, it is important to offer advice about how a person could eat *more* or *less* of a particular food group.

Remember that 'advice' is a noun whereas 'advise' is a verb. So, we give our friends *advice*, or we *advise* them about what they should do.

Similarly, 'practice' is a noun and 'practise' is a verb. So, we will *practise* the language we use to give advice. This *practice* will help you write better.

Ramon has decided to monitor his diet in order to be healthier. He has asked his friend Maria to help him to decide whether his diet is balanced or not. To help her do this, Ramon has recorded what he ate on one school day.

Breakfast	Lunch	Dinner
Cereal	Cheeseburger	Rice and fish
Toast with butter and jam	French fries	Ice cream
Cup of tea with three sugars	Chicken wings	Bottle of cola
Glass of orange juice	Large slice of chocolate cake	Glass of water
	Packet of crisps	
	Bottle of cola	

Maria looks at her friend's diet and makes the following suggestions. Select the correct words to complete her advice. (If you are not sure about the difference between *less* and *fewer*, look at the Language box below.)

Ramon, you have a diet that gives you a lot of energy but you eat far too much chocolate, cake, ice cream and crisps. You should eat fewer/less/more of these fatty foods because you will become obese.

There are no vegetables in your diet so you should increase/decrease the number of these that you eat to make sure that you get plenty of minerals in your body.

You have three sugars in your tea – I think that you should increase/decrease the amount of sugar that you have in your tea.

I am pleased that you drink water but if you want to have a balanced diet you should probably drink fewer/less/more water.

You get your vitamin C from the orange juice, but maybe if you *increase/decrease* the number of fizzy drinks that you consume, this would be better for you.

It is OK to treat yourself to some chocolate cake sometimes, but when you eat so many fats in one day, you should definitely try having a *smaller/larger* slice instead of such a big one.

You have plenty of carbohydrates from the bread, rice and potatoes. The meat and the fish supply the correct proportion of protein but please eat *fewer/less/more* vegetables and *fewer/less/more* fats.

Less and fewer

We use 'less' with *uncountable nouns*. These are, as it sounds, nouns that we can't or wouldn't normally count.

Examples are: rice, pasta, meat, chocolate, fish, water, money and so on. We can't say one water, two water, three water just as we can't say one money, two money, three money.

An example sentence: 'A lot of people should eat less chocolate.'

To count these words, we need a unit of measurement; for example, six bottles of water, 2000 Indian rupees, a portion of pasta, a bar of chocolate and two slices of meat.

We use 'fewer' with *countable nouns*; nouns we can count. A simple example is 'people'. We can count this noun; one person, two people, three people.

An example sentence: 'Fewer people eat healthily in many countries these days.'

Exercise 4.3 Carbohydrates, proteins and fats

> When you are learning about carbohydrates, proteins and fats, you will be expected to apply some of your knowledge about enzymes. You will practise doing this in this exercise.

Carbohydrates and fats must be broken down so that they can be used to release the energy that the body requires. Proteins are digested and help our bodies to grow and repair.

1 The word string below contains some of the key words related to the digestion of carbohydrates, fats and proteins. Separate the words and write them in the lines below.

carbohydratesfatsproteinsfattyacidsaminoacidsglycerollipaseproteasecarbohy
draseglucose

....

....

....

....

The name of the digestive enzyme is usually similar to the nutrient that it breaks down. *Carbohydr*ates are broken down by *carbohydr*ase – both words begin with '*carbohydr*.'

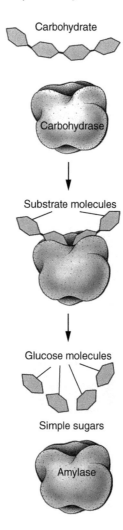

Carbohydrate

Carbohydrase

Substrate molecules

Glucose molecules

Simple sugars

Amylase

2 Use this knowledge to insert the names of **three** digestive enzymes from the word string into the table below.

Nutrient	Digestive enzyme	Product
carbohydrates		simple sugars
fats/lipids		fatty acids and glycerol
proteins		amino acids

3 Now that you have all of the information written down about the enzymes used in digestion, you can put these into sentences. Here is an example:

Carbohydrates are broken down by amylases to produce simple sugars.

As we saw in Unit 3, this sentence is passive. In this case it is the present simple passive and it is being used to describe a fact.

We start the sentence with the main term we want to define: *Carbohydrates*

Next, we choose the correct form of the verb *to be* (*is* or *are*):   *are*

Then, we add the past participle – the third form of the verb: *broken down*

Finally, we add the rest of our definition: *by amylases.*

Now write your own sentences for the other two examples in the table.

a Fats/lipids:

....

....

b Proteins:

....

....

The name of the digestive enzyme is often similar to the nutrient that it breaks down; such as protease for breaking down proteins. However, carbohydrates are broken down by a carbohydrase called amylase. You are expected to use amylase when referring to the enzyme that breaks down carbohydrates.

Exercise 4.4 Digestion key words

Digestion is a topic that will introduce you to a series of new words and names for parts of the body. Many words in this topic come from the same word families and it is important for you to select the correct word for the appropriate sentence. This task will help you to select the correct word and use it where suitable.

Many words have different forms and so we use them in different ways in sentences.

When you describe the *action* of something happening, you use a *verb*. For example, from the verb *to react*:

Different chemicals *react* with each other in our bodies.

The names of the *processes* taking place are *nouns*. For example:

When proteases break down proteins, this is a chemical *reaction*.

Many words connected with digestion can be used in these two ways. To form the noun from the verb, you can often use

verb + *-ion*

The sentences below outline some of the key words related to digestion. Choose the correct form – verb or noun – to complete each sentence. Cross out the incorrect option.

1 Ingestion/Ingest is when food and drink substances are taken into the body through the mouth.

2 Digestion/Digest is the breaking down of large, insoluble molecules into small, soluble molecules.

3 Molecules are absorbed/absorption through the wall of the alimentary canal.

4 Digested food molecules are assimilation/assimilated to the parts of the body where they are required.

5 Undigested food molecules are egested/egestion through the anus.

6 Muscles contract/contraction and relax to help food move along some parts of the alimentary canal.

7 Deaminate/Deamination is when the nitrogen part of amino acids is removed and occurs in the liver.

Exercise 4.5 The journey of digestion

In this exercise you will check that you know the names of the digestive organs. You will also practise writing a description of the journey of a piece of food through the alimentary canal from when it is eaten (digestion) to when it is removed from the body (excretion).

Digestion is the process of breaking down large, insoluble molecules into smaller, soluble molecules. Absorption takes place when the small, soluble molecules are absorbed by the blood through the small intestine.

The molecules are broken down through a series of processes in the alimentary canal and with help from other digestive organs.

1 Below is a list of digestive organs. Write each one next to the correct line on the diagram below.

large intestine	mouth	anus	stomach	rectum
oesophagus	pancreas	liver	small intestine	

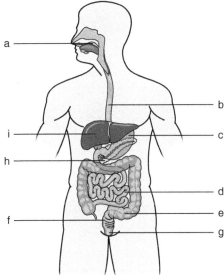

2 Now write an exciting story about the journey of a piece of food from when it is eaten to when it is removed from the body. You must include:

■ the names of all the **organs** that the food passes through using the diagram above to help you

■ information about **enzymes** and conditions in the body (amylase, lipase and protease)

■ names and characters to make your story as interesting as possible

■ any other **scientific content** that is important in digestion such as the role of the liver and pancreas in the digestion of food.

Here is an example of how the story could begin:

Miriam looked at her plate of food and thought about the journey that the food was going to take. Mariam put Rosalind Rice into her mouth where Rosalind saw her friend Sara Saliva. Sara Saliva had many enzymes to help break down Rosalind Rice into smaller pieces so that Miriam could swallow her. Rosalind was very happy as she went down the oesophagus towards the stomach. But she quickly got scared as the stomach was very dark and acidic. Luckily she escaped into the small intestine where she was...

....

....

....

....

....

....

....

....

....

....

....

....

....

....

....

....

....

....

5 Plant nutrition

This unit covers:

☐ how plants use inorganic substances to make organic substances
☐ photosynthesis equations – word and chemical
☐ the role of chlorophyll and chloroplasts
☐ the structure and function of a leaf
☐ experiments related to plant nutrition

Exercise 5.1 Inorganic to organic

The words 'organic' and inorganic' have different meanings in biology and everyday life. As a biologist, it is important that you have a clear idea what these terms mean, and how to use them.

Substances are either *organic* or *inorganic*.

1 Write the terms 'Organic' and 'Inorganic' in the correct places in the table headings.

> Think about what the **prefix** *in-* means.

contains both carbon and hydrogen, as well as other molecules	does not contain carbon and hydrogen
produced by living organisms	used by living organisms to build more complex materials

2 The substances below are all related to plant nutrition. Place them into the table to show whether each substance is inorganic or organic.

carbohydrates   **carbon dioxide**   **glucose**   **magnesium**   **oxygen**

proteins   **starch**   **water**

Organic substances	Inorganic substances

Exercise 5.2 Photosynthesis – word and chemical equations

> You need to understand the equations related to photosynthesis and be able to use them in your answers. This exercise will help you to remember the equations and be able to write about them.

1 a Complete the word and chemical equations for photosynthesis below.

carbon dioxide + ... $\xrightarrow[\text{chlorophyll}]{\text{sunlight}}$ .... + oxygen

.... + H_2O $\xrightarrow[\text{chlorophyll}]{\text{sunlight}}$ $C_6H_{12}O_6$ + ...

b Complete the definitions below:

Conditions   Reactants   Products

.... are substances that are present before a reaction takes place.

.... are things that are needed for a reaction to take place.

.... are substances that are present after a reaction takes place.

2 Look at the equations that you completed for photosynthesis. Identify the following:

a products: .... and ....

b reactants: .... and ....

c conditions: .... and ....

3 Use the exercises above to complete the summary:

Plants need carbon dioxide, ..., ... and chlorophyll to do

photosynthesis. Carbon dioxide and water are the .... After photosynthesis

has happened, glucose and oxygen are the .... A plant that has carried out

photosynthesis is said to have ....

Carbon dioxide .... the plant through small holes in the leaf called stomata.

This is also where oxygen .... the plant. Water is taken in by the roots

from the .... Glucose is an .... substance that the plant

will use to release energy for .... and repair.

Exercise 5.3 Limiting factors

A graph to show the rate of photosynthesis is useful for observing how different conditions can affect the rate. In this exercise you will practise how to describe a graph, as well as how to write about photosynthesis.

Sometimes the amount of sunlight, the concentration of carbon dioxide and the temperature might all be ideal for photosynthesis. If one of these is not ideal then this will be the limiting factor of photosynthesis. A limiting factor is something (such as the amount of light available) that limits the growth of the plant.

This graph shows how the concentration of carbon dioxide affects the rate of photosynthesis.

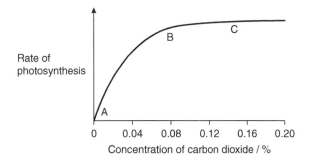

Look at these sentences. The first sentence is about the *gradient* of the graph (how steep the graph is). The second statement is about what the graph tells us.

> In section A, the gradient of the graph is steep.

> This shows that the rate of photosynthesis is increasing rapidly.

1 How does the graph change in section B?

In section B, the gradient of the graph is ....

This shows that the rate of photosynthesis is ....

2 Describe the graph in section C.

In section C, the gradient of the graph is ....

This shows that the rate of photosynthesis is ....

3 What is the concentration of carbon dioxide when the rate of photosynthesis begins to slow down? ....

4 What is the limiting factor for this particular plant? ....

Exercise 5.4 Leaf structure

The leaves of a plant are adapted to make sure that photosynthesis happens as efficiently as possible. You are expected to be able to **describe** how the structure of a leaf allows the leaf to do photosynthesis quickly and efficiently. In this exercise you will also think about structuring sentences correctly.

1   Below is a list of parts of a leaf. Each part has a specific function. Descriptions of each function are given, but the words are mixed up. Your task is to write the sentences with the words in the correct order.

Here is an example to help you:

upper epidermis: through. the sunlight This protects inner and cells to pass allows

This protects the inner cells and allows sunlight to pass through.

a   **palisade layer:** many cells of that near the top of contain a leaf

This is a layer ....

.... chloroplasts.

b   **stomata:** the holes at the of leaf that gases to allow diffuse in bottom

These are small ....

.... and out.

c   **waxy cuticle:** escaping water from the through leaf

This prevents ....

.... evaporation.

d   **chloroplast:** that chlorophyll sunlight for absorbs

This contains ....

.... photosynthesis.

e   **veins:** for xylem transporting and phloem vessels

These contain ....

.... substances.

f   **guard cells:** and close to gases allow in of the and out

These open ....

.... stoma.

2　Enter the missing labels in the spaces below the diagram of a leaf.

Look at your answers to question 1. Think about the function of each leaf part. Where would each part be in the leaf? What would it look like?

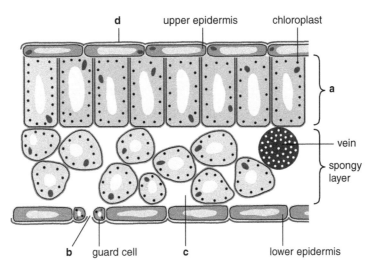

a　..

b　..

c　..

d　..

Exercise 5.5 Mineral deficiencies in plants

> The lack of minerals in a plant and how that plant looks are closely linked. This task will allow you to practise writing about these two factors together and enhance your knowledge of the mineral deficiencies.

Look at these sentences:

This plant looks healthy. *Therefore*, it must be getting everything it needs.

'This plant looks healthy' is an observation – something you can see. Because the plant is healthy, you know it is not lacking anything. 'The plant is getting everything it needs' is something you can *conclude* from the observation that it is healthy.

We can use the word *therefore* to connect a conclusion to an observation. 'Therefore' means 'for that reason'.

Plants take in minerals from the soil to allow them to make proteins and other substances that are vital for growth and good health. These minerals include:

■ nitrates

■ phosphates

■ potassium

■ magnesium.

If the plant does not get enough of these minerals, it will not grow as well or as healthily as a plant that does. The signs of an unhealthy plant are known as **symptoms** and you can use these to work out which mineral a plant is lacking.

Mineral	Symptoms of mineral deficiency
nitrates	lower leaves are yellow or dead, upper leaves are pale green
potassium	poor flower and fruit growth, yellow leaves with dead spots
phosphates	purple leaves and small roots
magnesium	lower leaves turn yellow

Look at these diagrams of plants with different mineral deficiencies.

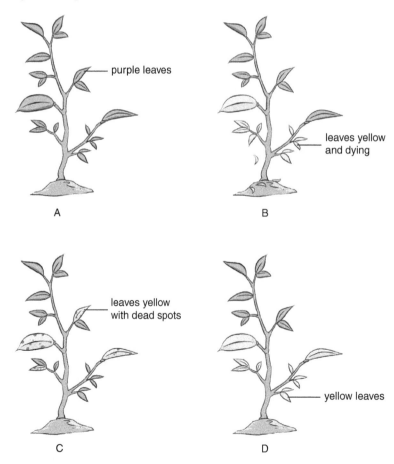

Use the table to decide what each plant is deficient in. Complete the sentences below to link your conclusions to the correct symptoms.

Here is an example to help you:

> Plant A has purple leaves. Therefore, it is deficient in phosphates.

1 Plant B ....

Therefore, it is deficient in ....

2 Plant C ....

Therefore, ...

3 Now write the two whole sentences for Plant D.

....

....

Exercise 5.6 Words to describe plants

This unit contains many English words that help to describe the structure or function of a part of plant nutrition. How well you understand these words will affect how well you understand the topic.

An example of this is describing a leaf as a food 'factory'. A *factory* is a place where things are made. A leaf uses raw materials to 'make' food for distribution around the plant.

1 Here are eight words connected with plants. The table below contains eight definitions. Write each word in the correct space in the table.

'v' means that the term is a verb, 'n' a noun and 'adj' an adjective.

absorb (v)   **factory**(n)   **guard** (n)   **limiting** (n)   **release** (v)

simple (adj)   **transport** (v)   **vessel** (n)

	Word	Meaning	Relation to plants	Extra information
a		a hollow container	xylem and phloem	transport water and minerals
b		take in or soak up	water taken in at roots	for example, roots . . .
c		allow to escape	the products of photosynthesis	for example, oxygen produced through photosynthesis is released
d		made of a single element	sugars such as glucose	the opposite of complex sugars
e		carry from place to another	water, minerals and sugars	movement of compounds
f		protects and controls	cells at a stoma	control the amount of carbon dioxide
g		where goods are made	leaf uses raw materials	food for distribution
h		sets a limit to	carbon dioxide, water and sunlight	. . . the rate of photosynthesis

2   Now use the information from the table above to create your own sentences about plants. You should aim to use the word, its meaning and how it is related to plants in your sentences. Here is an example to help you:

Factory: A factory is a place where things are made. A leaf uses raw materials to 'make' food for distribution around the plant.

a   guard

....

....

....

b   vessel

....

....

....

c absorb

....

....

....

d release

....

....

....

e transport

....

....

....

f limit

....

....

....

g simple

....

....

....

6 Transport in animals and plants

This unit covers:

- ☐ how substances are transported around animals and plants
- ☐ the structure and function of the human circulatory system
- ☐ the structure and function of blood
- ☐ the structure and function of the plant transport system

Exercise 6.1 Oxygen in the blood

It is essential that oxygen is moved around the body to allow organs and cells to release energy as part of the respiration process. This exercise will allow you to practise recognising and using some of the key words for the unit.

1 Read the paragraph below and enter the **bold** key words into the table below to match their meaning.

The mammalian **circulatory system** is a network of vessels and organs that allow blood to flow around the body. This is how substances such as **oxygen**, glucose, carbon dioxide and urea are moved around the body to where they are needed. This system relies on a central pump – the **heart**. The heart pumps the blood around the body via the large network of blood vessels. Blood that does not carry oxygen leaves the heart and travels to the **lungs**, where it will collect oxygen. This blood will then go to the left-hand side of the heart before being pumped all the way around the **body**. The blood will deliver the oxygen to the cells that need it, before completing this system by returning to the heart again.

	Key term	Meaning
a		where the blood collects oxygen
b		blood is pumped all around this by the heart
c		substance carried around the body in the blood
d		network of vessels and organs that pass blood around the body
e		the central pump of the body

2 Below is a diagram of the heart. Fill in the missing labels using the word string below. The paragraph at the beginning of this exercise may also help you here.

rightventricletobodytolungsfromlungsleftatrium

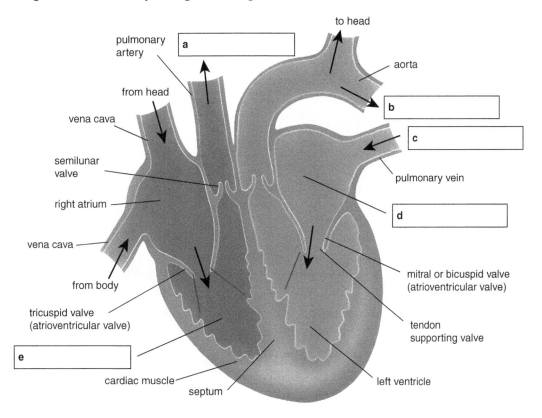

Exercise 6.2 Taking care of your heart

This task will focus on diseases related to the heart. You are expected to use sentences to link an unhealthy lifestyle to common diseases that affect the heart.

The causes of coronary heart disease are well known, and there are lots of things that a person can do to reduce the risk of coronary heart disease.

1 Some of the factors that increase the risk of heart disease are listed below. Unscramble the words and write the name of the factor that increases the risk of heart disease next to it.

a SMOG INK ....

b BITE SOY ....

c TIED ....

d RESTSS ....

e ICE GENTS ....

2 Ricardo has recently been to the doctor and admitted that he sometimes smokes a cigarette when he is stressed. Although he exercises regularly, Ricardo eats a lot of chocolate and other fatty foods. The doctor gave Ricardo some advice to reduce the risk of getting coronary heart disease.

Complete these two sentences that the doctor might have said to Ricardo for him to live a healthier and longer life.

a Ricardo should .... when he is stressed.

b Ricardo should .... his diet.

3 What does Ricardo do often that will reduce the risk of heart disease? Complete this sentence:

Ricardo often ....

Exercise 6.3 Blood vessels

Now that you have looked at the heart and how important it is, you will look at how different blood vessels help keep the blood flowing freely. This enables our bodies to get the nutrients and the oxygen that they need. You will also use prepositions to help describe the function of these vessels.

On, in, next to, in front of and behind, under and opposite are all **prepositions**. They are small words that, in this case, tell us where something is. Other prepositions may be connected to time – at 3 o'clock, on Thursday – to direction and so on. In question **1** you will use prepositions that show direction.

1 Look at the diagrams below and choose the missing word for each of the empty boxes using the list of words provided.

lumen   muscles   smooth   thick   thin   very small

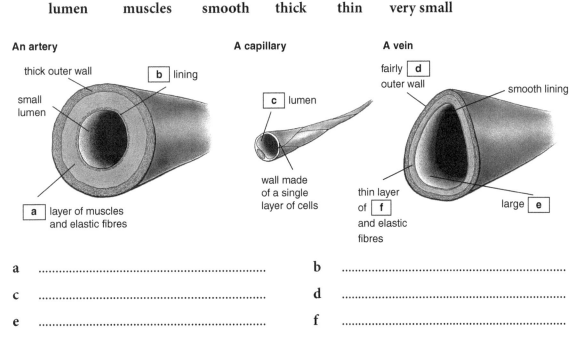

An artery

thick outer wall

small lumen

b lining

a layer of muscles and elastic fibres

A capillary

c lumen

wall made of a single layer of cells

A vein

fairly d outer wall

smooth lining

thin layer of f and elastic fibres

large e

a ....   b ....

c ....   d ....

e ....   f ....

The structure of each of these vessels depends on their function. The vessels that carry blood a long distance need to have very strong walls to withstand the high pressure of the blood when it leaves the heart. The blood that is flowing back to the heart can be easily pushed along wide vessels by contracting muscles.

2 Each vessel carries blood in a certain direction. Insert the prepositions into the gaps.

away   into   out   to   towards

Arteries carry blood .... from the heart and .... the cells

of the body at high pressure. Arteries divide .... smaller vessels until they

are capillaries. Capillaries take blood .... the cells and organs and allow

the nutrients and oxygen to diffuse .... The capillaries join together

again to form veins. Veins allow blood to travel .... from the cells and

back .... the heart.

Exercise 6.4 Effect of exercise on heart rate

A graph that shows how the heart rate changes over time before, during and after exercise can tell the story of what is happening in the body. This exercise will allow you to describe and explain what is happening during this process.

In Unit 2 there is a discussion of the **command words** describe and explain. We are going to do some more practice on these terms here.

Look back at the explanation in Unit 2 if you are not sure about what these words ask you to do.

Look at the graph below and complete the exercise that follows. The graph shows the heart rate of a man before, during and after exercise.

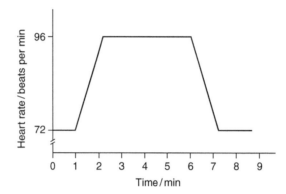

1 The following table contains statements. These statements either *describe* or *explain* what is happening in the graph above. Tick the correct box for each statement. The first one has been completed for you.

	Statement	Describe	Explain
a	The man has stopped exercising after 6 minutes.	✓	
b	The heart rate is increasing from 1 minute until 2 minutes.		
c	The heart is now beginning to pump blood faster around the body.		
d	The heart rate has stopped increasing at this point (after 2 minutes).		
e	The heart rate after 1 minute is 72 beats per minute.		
f	The heart rate is increasing from 72 beats per minute to 96 beats per minute.		
g	The man has completed his exercise and so the heart begins to pump less blood around the body.		
h	The heart rate has returned to its normal resting rate.		

You can combine descriptions and explanations.

Here is an example, using the description and explanation from the language box in Unit 2.

> Description: Chung's breathing rate increased rapidly after 3 minutes.
> Explanation: Chung's breathing rate increased because his muscles were using up oxygen for respiration and he needed to take more oxygen into his body.
> Combined sentence:
> Chung's breathing rate increased rapidly after 3 minutes because his muscles were using up oxygen for respiration and he needed to take more oxygen into his body.

2 Now produce a sentence of your own. Combine descriptions and explanations from the table in question **1** to produce a sentence that describes *and* explains what has happened.

....

....

....

....

Exercise 6.5 Transport in plants

> This exercise will allow you to learn the differences and similarities between two important vessels in plants – xylem and phloem. You will need to focus on recognising key words to complete this section.

Read the passage below that highlights some of the key structures and functions of the xylem and the phloem.

> Plants take in most of their water, minerals and nutrients from the soil and must transfer these to all of the different parts of the plant where they will be required.
>
> The two main vessels of transport – the xylem and the phloem – are responsible for this but have different structures and functions.
>
> The xylem is made up of hollow, dead cells to form hollow tubes. These vessels transport water and minerals in one direction from the roots to every part of the plant as they branch out through the leaves. The walls of xylem vessels contain lignin, which keeps the plant upright due to its strength.
>
> Phloem vessels have sieve plates to allow them to carry the nutrients made by the plant to where they are needed. As they could be needed at any part of the plant, phloem vessels are able to carry nutrients in both directions.
>
> Xylem and phloem vessels are usually found together in **vascular bundles**.

1 The word search below contains 11 different key words and phrases from the passage about xylem and phloem. Find these words and circle them on the word search.

X	V	V	A	S	C	U	L	A	R	S	O
Y	B	E	R	I	A	C	I	S	B	W	N
L	H	S	Z	E	W	E	G	V	A	W	E
E	A	S	X	V	B	R	N	R	W	A	D
M	A	E	G	E	U	T	I	R	B	T	I
E	V	L	B	T	B	U	N	D	L	E	R
J	U	S	E	F	M	M	L	O	O	R	E
M	I	N	E	R	A	L	A	R	T	U	C
P	R	L	B	O	O	M	E	R	S	T	T
R	E	N	U	T	R	I	E	N	T	S	I
V	C	Q	C	V	G	W	A	T	G	U	O
P	H	L	O	E	M	W	T	U	O	D	N

2 Some of the words relate to the xylem to the phloem or to both of the vessels. List the words that you found in the table below. One of them has been completed for you.

Xylem	Phloem	Both vessels
one direction		

3 Now use the words from the table above to write your own short paragraph about the structure and function of the plant transport vessels. You should explain:

■ the benefit of the structure

■ how the structure relates to the function of that particular vessel.

a xylem

....

....

....

....

....

b phloem

....

....

....

....

7 Respiration

This unit covers:

☐ how respiration releases energy
☐ the role of gas exchange in humans
☐ the process of breathing in and out
☐ how respiration, gas exchange and breathing are linked together

Exercise 7.1 Equations of respiration

The first stage of understanding respiration requires you to know what is required for respiration and what the products are.

This can be represented by word and chemical equations to show exactly what happens in the respiration reaction.

Once these equations have been understood and learnt – the rest of this topic will make more sense and be easier to understand.

Read the following text, then answer the questions below.

> Respiration is a chemical reaction that releases energy from nutrients such as glucose. Oxygen is required for the reaction to take place, and the products released are carbon dioxide and water. These are 'waste' products and are removed from the cell after respiration.

1 For respiration to take place, two reactants are required. Write the names of these reactants below.

....

2 The chemical reaction of respiration produces two waste products. Write the names of these products below.

....

3 Respiration has a third important product that is very useful for the growth and repair of our bodies. What is this useful product of respiration?

....

4 The respiration reaction can be summarised as an equation. Enter the answers to the questions above into the equation for respiration below.

.... + ... → .... + ... + energy

Exercise 7.2 Why we need respiration

Respiration is the release of energy from nutrient molecules. This energy has many uses for animals and plants: from allowing movement to cell division. In this exercise you must use nouns, verbs and adjectives correctly to describe what is happening during breathing and respiration.

In Unit 4 we discussed how some words can be used as both verbs and nouns.

Verb: Your chest *expands* when you breathe in.

Noun: The *expansion* of your chest makes room for air.

Here we introduce another way in which *some* **past participles** (the third form of a verb) can be used as an **adjective**. (An adjective is a word that says something about a noun.) For example:

I am *interested* in biology.

Here our past participle/adjective describes how someone feels – an interested person.

When they are *expanded*, your lungs contain more air.

Here the past participle/adjective describes how the noun is – an expanded lung.

1   This table contains some key words related to how animals and plants use energy. Complete the table by writing the correct form of the word in the empty cells.

Verb	Noun	Past participle/Adjective
contract	contraction	contracted
link	linking	linked
divide		divided
concentrate	concentration	
	transmission	*transmitted
	production	*produced

* Please note that transmitted and produced are only adjectives when they are used as compound adjectives – that is when there are two words. For example, 'a physically transmitted disease', 'a mass-produced car'.

2 Energy is required in organisms for the following processes. Use the correct word, in the correct form, from the table above to complete each sentence.

    a Internal body temperature must be kept constant, so heat is .... when the external environment is cold.

    b Damaged tissues grow and repair by the process of cell ....

    c Movement of the body is allowed by muscle ....

    d The movement of molecules against the .... gradient is required for active transport to take place.

    e Amino acids are .... together to form protein molecules.

    f Messages are sent around the body by the .... of nerve impulses to and from the different parts of the body.

3 In question **2**, circle the answers that are nouns. This shows that you know the difference between the nouns and the other word forms in the table.

Exercise 7.3 Aerobic and anaerobic respiration

> This exercise is aimed at giving you practice of writing word and chemical equations for respiration, as well as forming proper sentences when writing about them.

So far you have looked at *aerobic* respiration. This means that the reaction involves oxygen.

Sometimes, oxygen is not available. An organism may still be able to respire, and produce a small amount of energy, *without* oxygen. This is called *anaerobic* respiration.

Your understanding of the two types of respiration can be improved by using the different equations related to them:

    aerobic: glucose + oxygen → carbon dioxide + water + energy

    anaerobic: glucose → lactic acid + energy

Anaerobic respiration in humans is the breakdown of glucose into energy and produces **lactic acid**. These products are different from the products of aerobic respiration that you covered in Exercise 7.1.

> In Unit 2 we looked at describing differences. Here we will make more sentences that describe a contrast, this time using 'while' and 'whereas'. While and whereas mean exactly the same thing when used like this – in these sentences they mean something like 'but'.

1 Complete the table below to show the differences and similarities between aerobic and anaerobic respiration in humans. When writing about the differences, it is important that you mention both aerobic and anaerobic respiration.

Similarities	Differences
Both use glucose as a reactant.	Aerobic respiration produces carbon dioxide and water, whereas anaerobic respiration produces lactic acid.

The equations of aerobic and anaerobic respiration have a chemical version to show you the chemical make-up of each molecule involved.

Exercise 7.4 Gas exchange in humans

This exercise will look at how and where humans receive their oxygen for respiration. Humans breathe in air, which contains oxygen. The waste product of respiration – carbon dioxide – must also be released from the body.

This exercise gives you practice at constructing sentences about the part of the lungs that are essential for breathing and gas exchange.

Oxygen is taken into the body through the mouth and transferred to the blood at the lungs. There are several parts of the body that the oxygen molecules will pass through as a part of this journey.

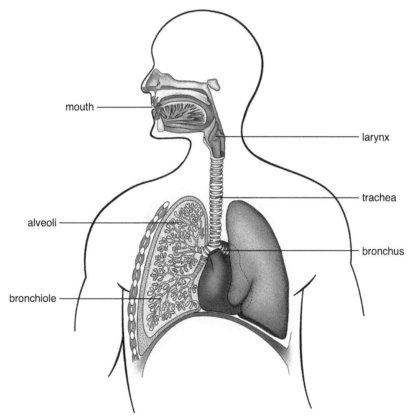

1   Use the words for each question below to construct a sentence using those key words. Here is an example to help you:

   breathe, mouth, oxygen

   We breathe in oxygen through our mouth.

   a   oxygen, passed, towards, lungs, trachea

   ....

   ....

b bronchus, divides, bronchiole, lungs

....

....

c gas, exchange, alveoli

....

....

2 The gas exchange system contains many words that can be confused when using them in the singular or plural. Place the words below into the correct column of the table. One row has been completed for you.

alveoli **bronchiole** **lung** **bronchi** **bronchus** **lungs**

bronchioles **alveolus**

Singular term	Plural term
lung	lungs

Exercise 7.5 Breathing in and breathing out

> The stages of breathing in and breathing out are set out in this task and will be a valuable tool for your understanding of this part of the topic.

Humans need oxygen for respiration and they need to remove waste products such as carbon dioxide. This happens by *inspiration* (breathing in) and *expiration* (breathing out).

Look at the diagram below, then answer the questions that follow.

The **prefixes** of these words make them easy words to remember.

In- is the prefix for **in**spiration; this is where we breathe **in**.

Ex- is the prefix for **ex**piration; this is where carbon dixoide **ex**its through breathing out.

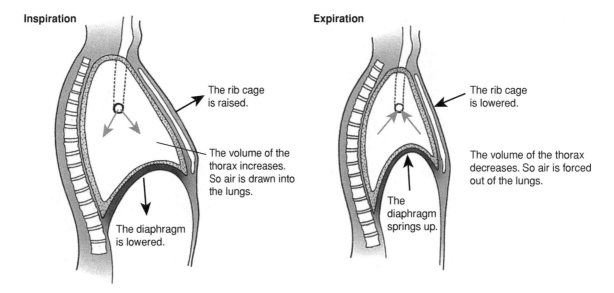

Inspiration

The rib cage is raised.

The volume of the thorax increases. So air is drawn into the lungs.

The diaphragm is lowered.

Expiration

The rib cage is lowered.

The volume of the thorax decreases. So air is forced out of the lungs.

The diaphragm springs up.

1 Complete the following paragraph by selecting the correct word from the options available to describe the stages of *breathing in*.

The muscles of the diaphragm contract/relax, which pulls the diaphragm upwards/ downwards. The external intercostal muscles contract/relax and pull the rib cage downwards/upwards. This increases/decreases the volume of the thorax and air rushes into/out of the lungs. The air rushes in because the pressure in the lungs is lower than that outside the body.

2 Complete the table below to show what happens to the body during *expiration*. The first one has been completed for you.

Part of the breathing system	What happens to this part
diaphragm	relaxes
external intercostal muscles	
rib cage	
thorax volume	
pressure in the lungs compared to outside the body	

3 Now, write a paragraph to describe what happens during expiration (breathing out). Use the information from the table in question **2**. The paragraph should be similar in structure to the one in question **1**.

....

....

....

....

....

....

....

....

....

....

8 Coordination and homeostasis

This unit covers:

☐ how humans and plants respond to different stimuli
☐ hormones and their responses
☐ the meaning and importance of homeostasis
☐ the human excretory system

Exercise 8.1 Responding to stimuli

A change in the external environment is a *stimulus* (plural: stimuli). This change begins a series of events that enable an organism to respond to the stimulus.

This first exercise will remind you of what our basic senses are and give you practice at reading a text and recognising key words. This is what you should be doing every time you read a text in a book or a question in an assessment.

Read the text below about our senses and answer the questions that follow.

> Jackson wakes up after hearing his alarm clock go off at 6.15 a.m. He touches the snooze button on his alarm clock and closes his eyes again. Suddenly, he hears footsteps approaching his room, and the door opens. Jackson's mother switches the light on; the light makes Jackson's eyes hurt. He can smell something delicious. As he gets used to the light, he can see his mother is holding a plate of pancakes and a cup of coffee – they smell amazing. Jackson eats his breakfast as quickly as possible. He can taste blueberries, syrup and lemon juice in the pancakes, and he washes this down with a mouthful of delicious-tasting coffee. Jackson is ready to get up now and enjoy a day of learning that lies ahead at school.

1 Underline all of the words in the text above that are related to your senses. For example, Jackson <u>hearing</u> his alarm clock is related to the sense of hearing.

2 There are five *senses*. Each sense is carried out by a certain *sense organ*. The names of the five sense organs are combined in the word string below. Separate the words in the string.

noseeareyetongueskin

3 Use the words from the word string to label this diagram of the sense organs.

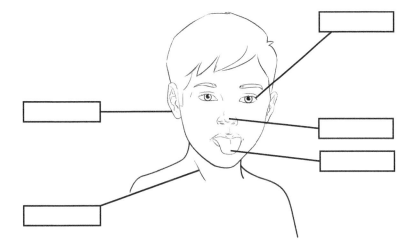

4 Use the diagram to decide which organ will respond to the different stimuli listed below. Complete the table with your answers.

Sensory organ	Stimuli detected
	vision, light
	hearing, balance
	smell, chemical
	taste, chemical
	touch, pain, temperature

Exercise 8.2 Reflex arcs

> This exercise will test your knowledge of the reflex arc and help you to get the order of the actions within the reflex arc correct.

A *reflex action* is an automatic response to a stimulus, for example pulling your hand away if you accidentally put it on something hot. In a reflex action, signals pass through three types of *neurone* (nerve cell) in a *reflex arc*.

This table introduces the three types of neurone that are involved in reflexes.

Type of neurone	Role in a reflex arc
sensory	carries electrical impulse from the receptors to the central nervous system
motor	carries electrical impulses from the central nervous system to the effectors (muscles or glands)
relay	carries electrical impulse across the spinal cord

1   Use the information in the table above to complete this diagram.

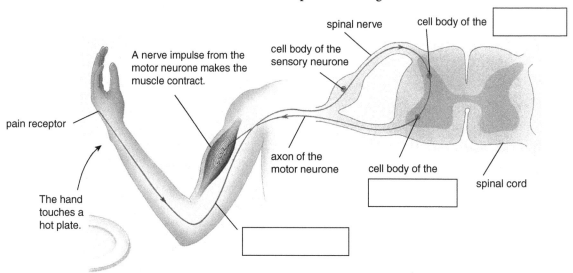

2   Look at these sentences. Each sentence has a mistake in it. Cross out the mistake, and write the correct sentence in the space below. Use the information in the diagram on the previous page.

Here is an example to help you:

A ~~reflex~~ detects a stimulus and converts it into an electrical impulse.

A receptor detects a stimulus and converts it into an electrical impulse.

a   The electrical reaction is carried to the central nervous system by a sensory neurone.

....

....

b   The electrical impulse is carried by a sensory neurone across the spinal cord.

....

....

c The electrical impulse is then carried away from the central nervous system along a relay neurone.

....

....

d The motor neurone carries the chemical impulse to an effector.

....

e An organ is a muscle or gland that carries out the response to the stimulus.

....

....

f A reflex action is a voluntary response to a stimulus.

....

g The plural of stimulus is stimuluses.

....

3 Read this text about two reflex actions.

A doctor may tap your knee to locate the tendon that lies beneath the kneecap. This tapping stretches the tendon, which produces the 'knee jerk' reflex action. This reflex action occurs because the muscles in the upper thigh contract to cause the leg to straighten. Without this reflex action, the body would not be able to support its own weight during walking.

When you eat some food, you rely on the automatic response of swallowing to ingest the food. When your throat makes contact with the food particles, it causes a muscle above the trachea (windpipe) to contract. This means that food cannot enter the trachea and it prevents damage to the lungs.

You can summarise the information in these paragraphs in a table like the one below. The information for the knee jerk reflex is already inserted. Complete the table by writing in the information for the swallowing reflex.

Reflex action	Stimulus	Response	Survival value
knee jerk	tendon stretched by tapping kneecap	upper thigh muscles contract	leg supports body weight when walking
swallowing			

Exercise 8.3 Nervous system versus endocrine system

In this exercise you will focus on the key words and ideas for the nervous system and the endocrine system. Remember that the endocrine system releases hormones and is a much slower response system than the endocrine system.

You will use adverbs to make sure that you are able to describe the differences between the two systems.

1 The *endocrine system* has similarities and differences with the nervous system, which you have just been looking at. Read the following passage and select the correct words to describe the endocrine system.

The endocrine system is made up of glands/tissue that secrete electrical impulses/hormones. Some of the glands produce hormones with similar names, which makes them easier to remember. An example of this is the thyroid gland, which produces the thyroxine/ adrenaline hormone. This hormone controls the metabolism of the body. The adrenal/ pituitary gland produces a hormone called adrenaline. Adrenaline is secreted into the blood and may make your heart/lungs beat faster when you are excited or scared. The testes are found in males/females and produce the testosterone/progesterone hormone. This hormone is important in reaching puberty and affects levels of aggression/sugar in men.

2 This table contains information about the endocrine system and the nervous system. Use your knowledge of these systems and the key words listed below to complete the table. Two of the answers have been completed for you.

electrical impulses   hormones   longer amount of time   neurones

nerve fibres   quickly   secretory cells   slowly

Feature	Nervous system	Endocrine system
made up of		
information transmitted by		
messenger sent along		blood vessels
speed at which impulse travels		
length of time the effect lasts for	short amount of time	

> **Adverbs** are used to give us, or add, extra information about a verb. They often end in *-ly* and can be used to describe what is happening in a biological process
>
> For example: Does an electrical impulse travel quickly or slowly?
>
> The electrical impulses travel very *quickly*.
>
> And: What is a volatile reaction? It is when chemicals react *violently*.

3 Now use the two adverbs from the box above to form **one** sentence about the two systems.

The first part of the sentence has been done for you:

In the nervous system, the impulse ....

but in the ....

....

4 Make other sentences in a similar way.

a The nervous system is made up of ....

while the ....

....

b In the endocrine system, information is ....,

whereas ....

c ....

....

d ....

....

Exercise 8.4 Homeostasis

> You will use this exercise to construct sentences that contain the correct word to describe what is happening in our bodies during homeostasis.

Homeostasis is the maintenance of a constant environment inside the body. This is crucial for organisms to continue to survive, grow healthily and work efficiently. Maintaining constant temperature, water levels and sugar levels ensures that our bodies can adjust to whatever the external conditions of the body may be.

1   Select the correct word to describe what happens when the body temperature is falling.

    When the external environment is cold, the body responds by doing the following:

    a   Shivering – rapid/slow contraction of muscles.

    b   Metabolism decreases/increases – releases more heat energy.

    c   Hair becomes flat/erect – traps an insulating layer of air at the skin surface.

    d   Capillaries near to the surface of the skin become wider/narrower – reduces the amount of heat lost.

    e   Sweat glands produce less/more – sweat to prevent evaporation.

> To write full descriptions, we can connect an explanation to an observation or fact using the word *which*. The part of the sentence following *which* is called a relative clause. For example:
>
> When humans are cold they start shivering, *which* is a rapid contraction of muscles.

2   The sentences in question **1a–e** are written in note form. Use 'which' to change each point into a proper sentence. Here is another example to help you:

    The metabolism increases, *which* releases more heat energy.

    a   Hair becomes ....

    b   Capillaries ....

    c   Sweat glands ....

Exercise 8.5 The human excretory system

> The many reactions that occur in our cells produce waste products that must be removed from the body. The excretory system ensures that this happens.
>
> This exercise will give you the opportunity to write about the excretory system to show how it works to keep the body working as it should do.

Excretion is the removal of toxic materials, waste products and other substances that are not required by the body.

1 On this diagram, four parts of the excretory system are indicated.

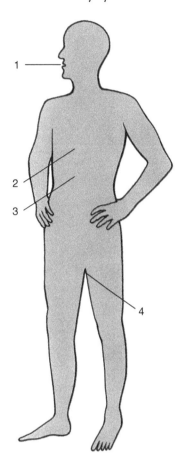

The four statements in the table below can be linked to the numbers in the diagram. They are also linked to the following organs.

kidneys   **liver**   **lungs**

Write the number that indicates where each excretory process takes place. You must also write the name of the excretory organ(s) involved in each process. You will need to use one organ name twice.

Statement	Number on diagram	Name of organ(s)
Carbon dioxide produced during respiration is excreted here.		
Bile pigments produced here are excreted in faeces.		
Urea (broken down proteins) excreted by this organ is passed out in the urine.		
Excess water and salts are removed by this organ.		

In Units 3 and 4 there is guidance on turning active sentences into passive sentences. To turn a passive sentence into an active one you follow the reverse process. Look at this passive sentence:

The carbon dioxide produced during respiration is excreted by the lungs.

This can be converted to the following active sentence:

The lungs excrete the carbon dioxide produced during respiration.

You choose between the active and passive depending on what you want to emphasise – the thing doing the action (the lungs – active) or the thing that receives the action (the carbon dioxide – passive).

2   Use the information from the table to construct active sentences about the excretory organs. You should turn the passive sentences from the table to active sentences. Use the language box to help you. In two of the answers you can use 'which' to make your sentences (as in Exercise 8.4, question **2**).

Finally, you will need to use the words 'kidneys', ' 'liver' and 'lungs' in your answers.

a   Bile pigments produced here are excreted in faeces.

The liver produces ....

....

b   Urea excreted by this organ is passed out in the urine.

....

....

c   Excess water and salts are removed.

....

9 Reproduction

This unit covers:

- asexual and sexual reproduction
- the reproductive organs in humans and plants
- the menstrual cycle and puberty
- sexual reproduction in flowering plants

Exercise 9.1 Asexual and sexual reproduction

This unit begins with a reminder about the different types of reproduction that you might have come across before in your biology studies. This task will compare the two types of reproduction and encourage you to identify the key words and differences between them.

Asexual reproduction results in the production of offspring that are genetically identical to the parent. This does not require gametes (sperm and ovum) and there is only one parent in this type of reproduction.

Sexual reproduction involves the joining together of the gametes to form a single, fertilised cell known as a zygote. This process produces offspring that are genetically different.

1   Use the information in the text above to complete the table below.

Feature	Asexual reproduction	Sexual reproduction
number of parents		two
are gametes present?		yes (sperm and ovum)
offspring	genetically identical	

2   Use the information in the paragraphs and table above and compare and contrast the two types of reproduction. You can use linking words like 'but', 'while' and 'whereas'. The first one has been started for you.

a   Number of parents

Asexual reproduction only requires one parent whereas sexual reproduction ....

....

b Gametes present

....

c Offspring

....

Exercise 9.2 The human sex cells

The structure and function of the human gametes (sperm and ovum) are vital to your understanding of the processes of sexual reproduction. These cells are specialised – they carry out a very specific job. This continues the work that you did in earlier units about specialised cells.

This task will remind you of those features, as well as helping you learn any new ones that you will need in this unit.

1 Look at the diagrams below and complete the following table to show how each part of the cell helps that cell to perform its job. The first one has been completed for you.

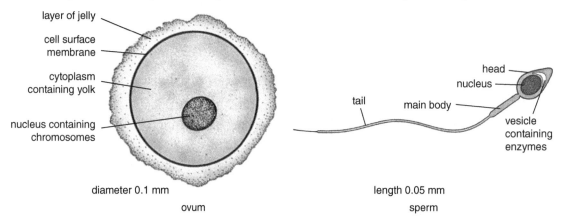

Feature of sex cell	Sperm or ovum?	Function in sex cell
nucleus	both	contains the genetic information in the chromosomes
		allows the cell to swim strongly towards the ovum
		is streamlined to reduce resistance when travelling
		prevents too many sperm penetrating the egg at one time
		contains many mitochondria to power the tail

2 Read the section of text below and insert the appropriate key word into the table to match the correct description. The scientific words from the text have been italicised to make them stand out as key words.

> The *sperm* must swim to the *ovum* and *fertilise* it within 24 hours of the egg being released from the *ovaries*. The ovum is released during *ovulation*, and travels along a tube called the *oviduct* where a sperm may fertilise it. The ovum is moved along the oviduct by *ciliated* cells and *peristalsis*.

Key word	Meaning
	female sex cell
	male sex cell
	the fusion of a sperm and an ovum
	tube that travels from the ovaries to the uterus
	the place where the ovum matures before release
	cells that contain small hairs to sweep the ovum along
	the monthly release of an ovum into the oviduct
	the contraction and relaxation of muscles to move the ovum along the oviduct

3 Two of the key words are parts of the female reproductive system. Write the names of these two parts in the spaces below.

....

....

Exercise 9.3 Puberty in males and females

Puberty is the period of time when a person reaches sexual maturity. This brings about many different changes in the body for males and females.

These changes include some of the following – changes in behaviour, changes in the hormones, as well as physical changes to the body. The changes enable the person to be physically able to reproduce.

This task will help you to recall the different changes and put them into a clear, concise sentence.

1   Underline all of the nouns in this diagram of the signs of puberty in males and females. There are five nouns missing from the diagram – write the correct noun into the empty spaces marked **a** to **e**.

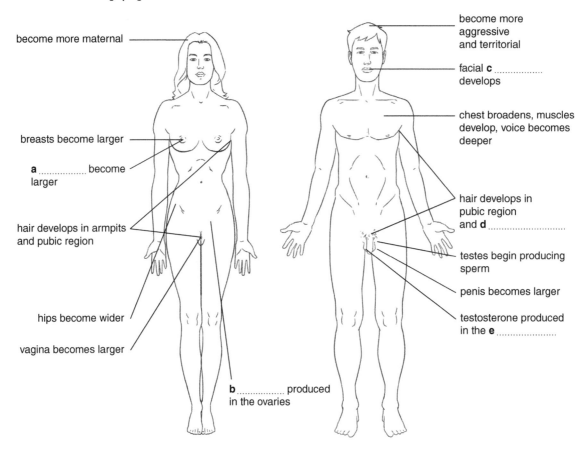

become more maternal

breasts become larger

a .... become larger

hair develops in armpits and pubic region

hips become wider

vagina becomes larger

b .... produced in the ovaries

become more aggressive and territorial

facial **c** .... develops

chest broadens, muscles develop, voice becomes deeper

hair develops in pubic region and **d** ....

testes begin producing sperm

penis becomes larger

testosterone produced in the **e** ....

2   One type of change that happens in puberty is changes to the *hormones* (special chemicals) in our body. Complete the following sentences to describe these hormonal changes. Use the diagram in question **1** to help you.

a   Women produce .... in the ....

b   Men ....

3   *Physical change* means changes that happen to the body. Look at the diagram in question **1** and write the physical changes in the correct column.

Women	Men

4 *Behavioural change* means changes that happen to how a person acts or feels. Use the diagram in question **1** to write the behavioural changes in the correct column.

Women	Men

5 *Hormonal changes* are the reason other changes happen. We say that hormonal changes *cause* the other changes.

Complete the sentences about how hormones cause other changes.

a Oestrogen production in women causes physical changes like ....

.... and behavioural changes like

....

b Testosterone production in ....

....

....

Exercise 9.4 Fertilisation and implantation

The information learned so far in this unit will help prepare you for the two stages of sexual reproduction that we will look at now.

This exercise will look at the stages of the processes of fertilisation and implantation and give you practice at using the correct verb forms to describe what is happening in these important processes.

In this exercise where you are completing definitions, it is important to get your verb agreement right. As you know, verb agreement works like this: I like, he/she/it likes, you like, we like, they like.

It is more complicated when you are given the noun (or noun phrase) and not the pronoun. When this happens, you must decide which pronoun matches the noun.

For example:

The/a zygote – This is one thing and so matches to the pronoun 'it' and so the verb is 'forms'.

The/a zygote (it) is a cell that **forms** when **two gamete cells** (they) **join.**

You will also see definitions that don't use 'the' or 'a/an' at the beginning. In this case the verb agreement changes. For example, zygotes is not one thing but all zygotes and so matches the pronoun 'they':

Zygotes (they) **are** cells that form . . .

Look at the diagram below and use the key word list to complete the sentences in the text that follows.

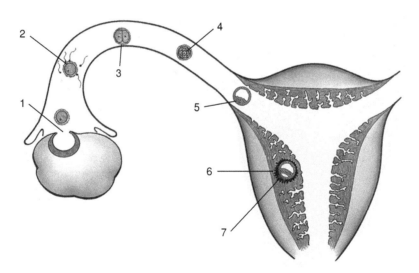

Use these verbs in the correct form to complete the paragraph.

reach   divide   fuse   release   form   support   sink   move   form

First, ovaries .... a mature ovum into the oviduct. Then, sperm

.... the ovum and they .... to form a zygote. We call this

fertilisation. Next, the zygote .... This type of cell division is mitosis. A

ball of cells .... after many divisions. After that, the ball of cells ....

down the oviduct while dividing. We now call this an embryo. Embryos ....

into the soft lining of the uterus. We call this implantation. At this stage, the placenta

.... and .... the developing embryo.

Exercise 9.5 Sexual reproduction in plants

Flowering plants can reproduce asexually as well as sexually. This happens when *pollen* (containing the male gametes) is transferred from one plant to another.

The first question in this section will help you to link the reproductive parts of the flower to their function. The second question will assess your ability to describe the process of sexual reproduction in plants.

1   Use the diagram to work out which part of the flower performs which function. The description of the function will contain clues as to which part of the plant it is referring to.

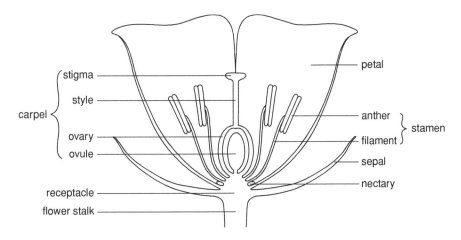

Part of the plant	Function
	platform for pollen to land on
	the male part of the flower that is made up of the anther and the filament
	brightly coloured and scented to attract insects
	green part of the plant and protects the flower
	main stalk that holds the stigma in place
	hollow chamber from which the ovules develop
	female gamete found inside the ovary
	contains pollen grains and located at the end of the filament
	long stalk that holds the anther in place

2   Read the following statements about sexual reproduction in flowering plants.

Pollen that is released from an anther lands on the stigma – *pollination* occurs.

The male and female gametes are haploid (contain half of the number of chromosomes).

Pollen tube forms down the style.

Delivers male gamete to the female gamete in the ovule.

Pollen tube finds gap in micropyle at the bottom of the style.

Fertilisation happens – the male and female gametes fuse together.

Zygote develops into an embryo and then a seed.

The statements have not been written as proper sentences. The first sentence should read:

The pollen that is released from an anther lands on the stigma and pollination occurs.

Your task is to write a paragraph about sexual reproduction in flowering plants by changing the statements above into proper sentences.

We have already looked at linking devices for comparing and contrasting. In this exercise you should use linkers for 'addition', that is adding ideas logically in a sequence. You can see an example in Exercise 9.4.

You should organise your paragraph using linkers such as 'First', 'then', 'next', 'after that', 'as a result of this', 'this means' and so on. It makes your paragraph much easier for the reader to follow and helps you organise your thoughts logically.

....

....

....

....

....

....

....

....

....

....

....

....

....

....

....

....

....

....

....

....

10 Inheritance and evolution

This unit covers:

- ☐ the inheritance of chromosomes and genes
- ☐ mitosis and meiosis
- ☐ how to use a genetic cross to predict genetic variation
- ☐ natural selection and evolution

Exercise 10.1 Structure of a chromosome

The understanding of this unit can be assisted by a good knowledge of the technical terms related to a chromosome. This exercise will help you to understand the technical terms related to a chromosome and basic inheritance key words.

Your task is to read the text available and find the relevant key words to show that you are beginning to understand how they are used.

1 Separate the words in the word string below and write them in the spaces available. The first one has been completed for you.

chromatidchromosomegeneDNAallelegenotypephenotypehomologouscentromere

...............chromatid...............   ....

....

....

....

....

2   Read the text and select the missing word from the options available.

The two chromosomes from the mother and the father contain genetic information and are called homologous chromosomes. A chromosome is a string/protein of DNA that contains all of the genetic/medical information for that cell. A gene is a length of this DNA that we often refer to as the 'bundle/unit of inheritance' and carries the code for specific proteins. A homologous chromosome is made up of two chromatids that are joined together at the end/middle by a centromere. Each gene has two different versions which can be expressed – these versions are called alleles. These alleles and your genes make up your characteristics/nucleus and when this information is shown as an observable characteristic it is known as the phenotype.

Answer the questions below that are related to the text above.

3   Which word in the text suggests that the genetic information will carry the code for one type of protein?

....

4   Which adjective shows that there may be more than one type of the same gene?

....

5   What is meant by the word *observable*?

....

6   Give an example of an observable characteristic.

....

7   What is the scientific key word for the different versions of a particular gene?

....

8 Use the information from your answer in the text above to label the diagram below. There are four words from the text that should be used to label the three blank boxes on the diagram.

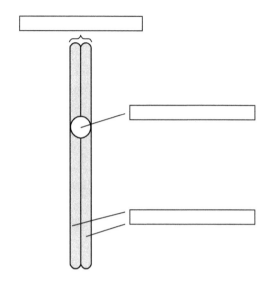

Exercise 10.2 Mitosis and meiosis

Cell division relies on two key processes – *mitosis* and *meiosis*. This exercise will help you to clearly distinguish between the two types of cell division.

You will be expected to look at diagrams of mitosis and meiosis and be able to describe what is happening at the different stages.

1 Look at the diagram of mitosis below and complete the sentences that follow. You should aim to *describe* what is happening at each stage.

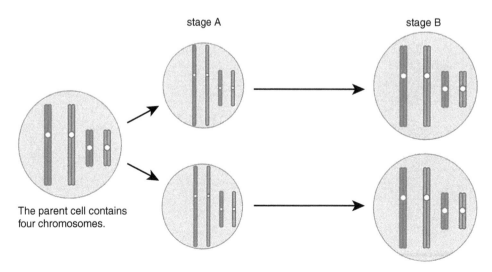

stage A   stage B

The parent cell contains four chromosomes.

a How many chromosomes does the parent cell contain at the beginning?

....

b Describe what happens to the chromosomes in stage A.

....

c The chromatids from each chromosome go into the daughter/father cell in stage A.

d What word would describe what has happened to the chromosomes in stage B? They have been ....

e How many daughter cells have been produced by mitosis?

....

2 The diagram below summarises what happens during meiosis. Your task is to use the diagram to answer the questions that follow to show that you are able to select the correct words when describing meiosis.

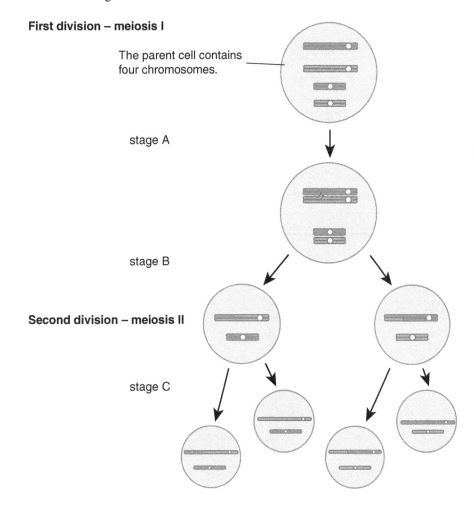

a Homologous chromosomes pair together during stage A. How many chromosomes make up a pair?

....

b How many daughter cells are present at stage B?

....

c What happens to the pair of homologous chromosomes during stage B?

....

d During stage C, the chromosomes separate into two chromatids. Where do these chromatids go to?

....

e How many daughter cells are produced at the end of one round of meiosis?

....

Exercise 10.3 Dominant and recessive alleles

Each cell in the body carries two different versions of a gene for any given characteristic. The two different versions are called *alleles*. You might carry genetic information for the brown phenotype eye colour but have an allele for blue eyes and an allele for brown eyes.

This task will give you practice at using the terms 'dominant' and 'recessive' and lead into other key terms for this part of the unit. You will need to read the information carefully in order to answer the questions that are in this exercise.

Meet Melissa and Jordan.

Melissa has blue eyes. She has two alleles for blue eyes.

Jordan has brown eyes. He has one allele for brown eyes and one for blue eyes.

Jordan's allele for blue eyes has not had an effect on his observable characteristics. This is because he *also* has an allele for brown eyes.

1 Complete these sentences:

The allele for .... eyes is *dominant* over the

allele for .... eyes. The allele for ....

eyes is *recessive*.

> In everyday English, *dominant* means 'has power over'.

2 We say that Melissa is *homozygous* and Jordan is *heterozygous*.

   a What does the prefix *homo-* mean? ....

   b What does the prefix *hetero-* mean? ....

   c What does it mean if someone is *heterozygous*? ....

   ....

> We can use single letters as *symbols* for different alleles.
>
> We use *upper case* letters for dominant alleles. For example, we can call the allele for brown eyes 'B'.
>
> We use *lower case* letter for recessive alleles. For example, we can call the allele for blue eyes 'b'.

3 Below are several pairs of alleles. State whether each one is homozygous or heterozygous. Here is an example to help you:

   HH   homozygous

   a Hh   ....   **d** XY   ....

   b hh   ....   **e** XX   ....

   c Bb   ....   **f** Ww   ....

4 Melissa and Jordan have a daughter. She has brown eyes.

   a What allele has she received from Melissa? ....

   b How do you know this?

   ....

   c What allele has she received from Jordan? ....

   d How do you know this?

   ....

   ....

You can work out the chances of Melissa and Jordan having a child with blue or brown eyes.

If you know the alleles for each gene of each parent in sexual reproduction, it is possible to predict the probability of the phenotype of their offspring. Look at the example below.

You can use a *genetic cross* to work out what offspring could be produced.

		mother	
		b	b
father	B		
	b		

By combining the different allele combinations in the table you will produce the following:

		mother	
		b	b
father	B	Bb	Bb
	b	bb	bb

5 This genetic cross shows that the offspring of Jordan and Melissa would have a

.... % chance of having blue eyes.

6 If the offspring has brown eyes, will it be homozygous or heterozygous?

....

7 Complete your own genetic cross below for two heterozygous parents. The parents are heterozygous for black hair (B) and brown hair (b).

		mother	
		B	b
father	B		
	b		

8 Circle the offspring that would have black hair.

9 Write a sentence that states what the chances are of offspring of these parents having black hair.

....

....

Exercise 10.4 Codominance and blood groups

Sometimes a pair of alleles is neither completely dominant nor completely recessive. This is called *codominance*. If an organism is completely dominant for two different alleles, this may produce a new phenotype in that organism. The inheritance of blood is an example of codominance.

This exercise will use your knowledge of inheritance gained so far to learn about the effects of codominance. You will then be able to produce a sentence about codominance towards the end of the exercise.

The three available alleles for blood groups are A, B and o.

1 a Write down which of these alleles are dominant in the space below.

....

b The codominance of these alleles will produce a fourth phenotype for blood group. Complete the table to show what this phenotype will be.

Alleles	Phenotype
AA or Ao	blood group ....
BB or Bo	blood group ....
	blood group o
AB	blood group ....

c Circle all of the genotypes that are homozygous in the table.

2   Your task is to produce a genetic cross to investigate the different combinations of blood groups that an offspring may express.

    a   Complete the genetic cross to show the offspring that could be produced for parents with the genotypes AA and Bo.

		mother	
		B	o
father	A		
	A		

    b   Write a sentence that explains the probability of the offspring having the blood group AB. You should use the following key words in your sentence: codominant and phenotype.

    ....

    ....

    ....

Exercise 10.5 Darwin and evolution

Charles Darwin published a book called *On the Origin of Species* that contained his theory of evolution. This theory forms the basis for our way of thinking even today – the book was published in 1859!

This exercise will introduce you to Darwin and some of his key ideas. You will use these ideas to produce a piece of writing that covers natural selection and evolution.

Read the following text about Darwin and his theories.

Darwin proposed that there was some *variation* within a species that would allow them to better adapt to their environment. Darwin also noted that only the organisms that were well adapted to their environment would survive. This theory is commonly known as *survival of the fittest*.

Darwin suggested that well-adapted organisms would pass on their characteristics to their offspring and were more likely to reproduce than those that are not well adapted. This means that those organisms that are not well adapted will decrease in the population and the remaining population would be stronger and better as a whole.

1 Use the information provided above to complete the spaces in the table below.

Key word/term	Definition
	a system of ideas and principles used to explain something
	adjusts to new conditions
	a particular feature of a thing or an organism
variation	
environment	

2 Look at the diagrams below and answer the following questions.

The two moths above both live in an area where the trees are darkly coloured as a result of pollution at a nearby factory. The number of moths was recorded over a period of time and it was noted that the population of some of the moths decreased.

a The population of *which* type of moth decreased? ....

b Why did the population of this type of moth decrease?

....

....

c Why were the trees a dark colour?

....

....

3 Look at the illustration below.

a The lions in the illustration above are well adapted to survive in their environment. They are predators and will use all of their physical characteristics to hunt and kill their prey. Label the illustration with at least two of the characteristics that the lion has in order to survive.

b Your task is to write a paragraph about how the lion is adapted to its environment. You should use the features that you have labelled and write them as proper sentences. Link your observations to an explanation when writing your paragraph.

In your paragraph you can write your sentences in two different ways to link your observation to the explanation, that is the fact to the reason or purpose:

Observation		**Explanation**
The lion can catch its prey easily	because/as	it has very strong legs.
	('because' and 'as' here refer to the reason)	
The lion has very strong legs	so that/in order that	it can catch its prey easily.
	('so that' and 'in order that' refer to the purpose)	

....

....

....

....

....

....

....

....

....

....

c What would happen to the population of the lions if they did not have these features?

....

....

....

....

11 Ecology

This unit covers:

- ☐ organisms and their environment
- ☐ energy in food chains and food webs
- ☐ the effect of the increasing human population on the environment
- ☐ protecting the environment from the harmful effects caused by humans

Exercise 11.1 Ecological key words

This unit contains many key words that are crucial to your understanding of it. This first exercise is aimed at introducing you to any new terms, as well as improving your understanding of the ones that you may already be familiar with.

1 The word string below contains words that are an important part of this topic. Separate the words and write them in the space below. The first word has been done for you.

environment|ecologyhabitatpopulationcommunityecosystemenergyfoodchainfoodweb

.... environment ....

....

....

2 The answers to question **1** can be inserted into the table below. You must match the meaning of the word to its definition.

Word	Definition
habitat	the area where an organism lives
	the number of organisms of the same species living together in the same area at the same time
	a network of food chains connected together to show the flow of energy in that ecosystem
	shows the flow of energy from one organism to the next
	the study of organisms and their environment
	all of the organisms of different species that occupy the same habitat
	this is required for organisms to grow healthily
	an area that contains all of the organisms and their environment
	the surroundings of an organism

Exercise 11.2 Food chains and food webs

> Energy from the Sun is passed along a *food chain* as animals consume other organisms. The food chain shows how the energy is passed from one level to another.
>
> This exercise will introduce you to some of the key terminology for the different roles that plants and animals have within food chains. You will also practise your use of conditionals to describe the effects of sudden changes in a food chain.

A food chain shows the flow of energy between organisms. They usually begin with a plant called a *producer*. Animals follow next in the food chain and they are the *consumers*.

Think about your schools; many of you will have attended primary (same as Elementary) school before secondary (same as Middle and High) school. Some of you will know that primary means 'first' and secondary follows primary. You can use that knowledge to make sure that you always identify the correct type of consumer in your answers. Primary consumers eat the producers and secondary consumers eat the primary consumers, and so on.

1 Observe the food chain below and use the information above to enter the following words into the boxes.

primary consumer (grasshopper)   **secondary consumer (flycatcher)**

producer (plants)

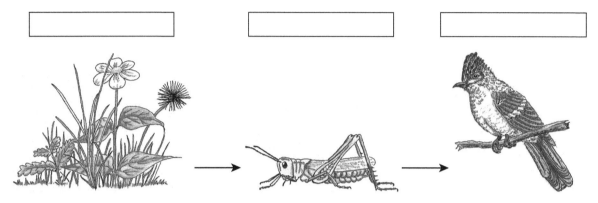

2 Use this information to complete the following sentences.

The .... is the producer in this food chain. The producer gets their

energy from the .... before it is passed along the food chain. The plants

are eaten by the .... consumer, which in this case is the ....

The flycatcher is the secondary .... and gets its energy by eating the

grasshopper.

3 Food chains are generally short as the organisms lose energy during respiration and other reactions. Some of the energy is 'lost' to the atmosphere and is considered to be wasted. *Food chains* can be linked together to form *food webs*. Look at the food web below and answer the questions that follow.

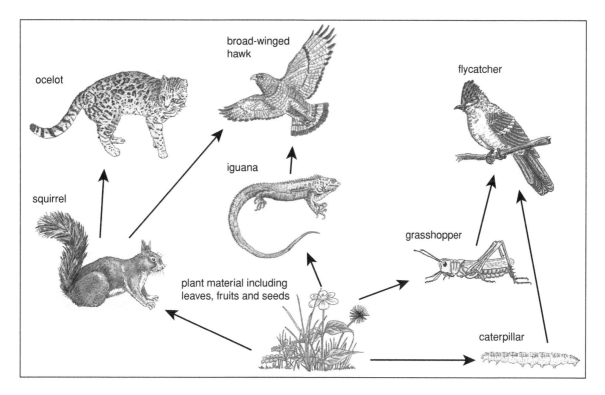

a How many producers are in this food web? ....

b How many primary consumers are in this food web? ....

c Name all of the primary consumers that you have counted.

....

d What level of consumer is the ocelot? ....

4 If an organism within a food web suddenly increased or decreased in number, then this would have an effect on the other organisms in the food web. For example, if the number of grasshoppers dramatically decreased, then the flycatcher would struggle to get enough energy and may decrease in number. Similarly, the number of caterpillars may decrease because the flycatcher would have to consume more of them to survive.

In science, and other subjects, if we imagine the likely effect of something that hasn't actually happened, then we are hypothesising. In English, a useful structure for doing this is the second conditional. This is:

If .... + ... past simple, (then) .... would   +   infinitive ....

If the number of grasshoppers decreased, then the flycatcher would struggle to survive.

The past simple is the second form of the verb: decrease, decreased, decreased

take, took, taken

The infinitive is the basic form of the verb – it never changes (it is infinitely the same).

Imagine that all of the iguanas suddenly increased, died or moved away from this particular ecosystem. What would happen? Complete the second conditional sentences to show what effect this would have on the other organisms in the food web.

a   If the population of iguanas increased, then the population of broad-winged hawks would ....

b   If the population of iguanas decreased, then the population of plants ....

....

c   .... of iguanas decreased, then the .... of

grasshoppers ....

d   Write your own full sentence using the second conditional to describe the effect of a change in iguana population on the population of the squirrels.

....

....

Exercise 11.3 The human population

The population of the world has recently increased to over 7 billion people. This is due to people living longer, and the rising number of babies being born. This has been possible because of improvements in diet, farming and medicine.

Unfortunately, this is having an effect on the environment as resources are needed to feed and shelter so many people.

This exercise will begin by looking at how and why the human population is increasing so fast.

Look at the graph below of human population and how it has changed in the past 2000 years.

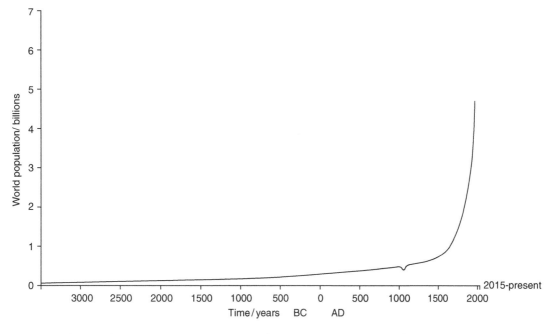

1   Your task is to describe what happens to the population in the following time periods. You should use words such as the following to describe the trends in the graph. Note (v) is verb, (adv) adverb, (adj) adjective and (n) noun (see Exercise 8.3 for help with adverbs).

decrease (v)   increase (v)   slowly (adv)   rapidly (adv)   at a steady rate (adj/n)

Between the years 0 and 500 AD

... the population is increasing at a steady rate ....

a   Between the years 500 and 1500 AD

....

b   Between the years 1500 and 2000 AD

....

2   There are many reasons why the population is increasing. Read the following paragraph and complete the task that follows.

The human population has increased to over 7 billion people in recent years and most of this growth has taken place during the past 200–300 years. The death rate has been decreasing during this time as there is less disease killing large numbers of people. This has been due to the advancement of modern medicine and the training of doctors and nurses. People have been getting *immunised* – which protects against disease – and so fewer people die from diseases that would have killed years before. The quality and quantity of food have improved too, as farming methods are able to produce large quantities of food at a lower cost. The diets of people have also improved and this is contributing to people living much longer. It was not that long ago when people would expect to live to their thirties or forties but now some people live well past 100 years old!

Select the **three** most important statements to summarise this paragraph. Write them in the space below.

....

....

....

....

....

....

3 The increase in human population has led to an increase in pollution. Air and water are becoming more polluted, and habitats and species are being destroyed. This is due to the demands of the increasing population as they require more food and shelter.

Complete the following sentences using the options available to get an overview of the effect of the increasing human population.

More people means more cars, more planes, more fuels being burnt. The gases produced in burning fossil/petrol fuels are being released into the atmosphere. This is contributing to the decrease/increase in air pollution. Rivers and lakes are being polluted by toxic chemicals, pesticides and oil spills. The decreased/increased demand for farming and the space needed for homes and factories are destroying habitats and the people/species that live within those habitats.

Exercise 11.4 Global warming and acid rain

Two of the biggest dangers to the well-being of our planet are *global warming* and *acid rain*.

Global warming is the increase in the temperature of Earth due to the heat energy that is being trapped inside the atmosphere.

Acid rain is caused by gases that are turning rainwater acidic. Rain is usually slightly acidic but these gases are causing the rain to become more and more acidic. This causes damage to plants, animals and even buildings.

This task will look at the causes and effects of these two problems and what could be done to prevent more damage in the future.

Read the paragraph below.

> Acid rain is caused by sulfur oxides and nitrogen oxides being released during combustion (burning) of fossil fuels. The oxides produced dissolve in water in the clouds and fall as acid rain. Acid rain causes the acidity of soil to increase, and vital minerals are washed out. Plants cannot take in these vital nutrients and will die or not grow properly. The minerals that are washed out end up in rivers and lakes where they are poisonous to organisms that live in the water. These organisms may also die as a result of this.

1 The paragraph contains the following:

- causes of acid rain – that is, why it happens

- effects of acid rain – that is, the result of it happening.

Find the causes of and effects of acid rain in the paragraph and write them in the table below.

Causes of acid rain	Effects of acid rain
sulfur oxide released into atmosphere	pH of soil increases

Global warming is caused by greenhouse gases (carbon dioxide, methane, chlorofluorocarbons (CFCs)) trapping heat energy in the Earth's atmosphere. The heat energy cannot radiate out of the atmosphere as it should do.

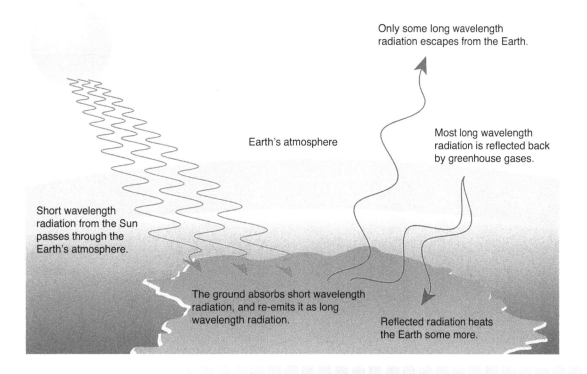

The effects of global warming are:

- extreme climates – hurricanes, heavy rainfall

- water evaporates from fertile areas to form deserts

- polar caps melt which lead to rising sea levels and flooding.

Many people and governments are campaigning to fight global warming and have come up with the following ideas to limit the effects of global warming:

- burn fewer fossil fuels

- cut down fewer forests and trees (which take in carbon dioxide from the atmosphere)

- replant forests that have been cut down previously

- stop using CFCs (found in aerosols and refrigerators)

- collect methane from landfill sites.

2 Your task is to select **two** of the ideas for limiting global warming and link them to the causes of global warming that will help to reduce it. You should practise your use of second conditionals in forming your sentences to show how an action would have an effect. An example has been done for you. Write your examples in the spaces below.

If we burned fewer fossil fuels, we would release fewer greenhouse gases into the atmosphere.

....

....

....

....

Answer key

1 Classification

Exercise 1.1 Characteristics of living organisms

1   movement; respiration; excretion; organism; sensitivity; nutrition; growth; reproduction

2   **a**   organism
    b   excretion
    c   growth
    d   movement
    e   nutrition
    f   reproduction
    g   respiration
    h   sensitivity

Exercise 1.2 Unusual plurals

1   genera; genus

2   fungi; fungus

3   species; species

Exercise 1.3 Constructing a key – writing opposites

1   mammal

2   The organism does not feed its young on milk.

3   The organism has a moist, smooth skin.

4   fish

5   The organism does not have gills and fins.

Exercise 1.4 Describing organisms

1   *Homo*

2   Any four from: fur, hair, mammary glands, whiskers and teeth (incisors and canines)

3   Placenta, diaphragm, a heart with four chambers and well-developed brains

4   homeothermic

5   A well-developed brain allows mammals to make decisions about sources of food and possible dangerous prey. (Any other sensible answer about communication or decision-making is acceptable.)

6   Incisors and canines allow mammals to cut and tear food/prey for nutrition/nutrients.

Exercise 1.5 Using prefixes to define words

1   di-; two/twice

2   in-; not

    ex(o)-; outside of

3   mono-; one

4   chloro-; green

Exercise 1.6 Kingdom to species – using the key words in context.

1   species; binomial; *Bos;* family; plants; order; Mammalia; backbone; phylum; kingdom

2   *Your answer should include:*
    – *the seven different classification groups that your chosen animal belongs to.*
    – *a characteristic that explains why the animal is in a particular group, for three different groups. An example is the explanation that the cow is part of the Bovidae family because it is herbivorous.*
    – *your sentences.*

2 Cell structure and function

Exercise 2.1 The parts of a cell

1   **a**   chloroplast
    b   large vacuole
    c   plasma membrane
    d   cell wall
    e   cytoplasm
    f   nucleus
    g   chlorophyll

2

Plant cell only	Plant cell and animal cell
large vacuole	plasma membrane
chloroplast	*nucleus*
chlorophyll	*cytoplasm*
cell wall	

Exercise 2.2 Comparing cells

1   The plant cell and the animal cell *both contain* a nucleus.

2   The root hair cell has a large vacuole but *the nerve cell does not.*

3   The ciliated hair cell has small hairs to trap mucus, but *the muscle cell does not.*

4   The red blood cell does not contain a nucleus, but *the nerve cell does.*

5   *For example*:
The animal cell and the plant cell both contain cytoplasm.
The plant cell contains chloroplasts, but the animal cell does not.
Make sure your sentence follows one of these patterns.

Exercise 2.3 Organisation of cells

1   organ

2   cells

3   organs; system

4   cell

5   cells

6   cells

7   a tissue; cells

8   tissue

9   organ

Exercise 2.4 Describing diffusion

1   higher; into; diffuse; partially

2   *This example answer is structured in the same way as the paragraph in question 1. You might have structured your answer differently.*
The concentration of oxygen molecules is lower outside the cell than inside. This will cause the molecules of oxygen to move out of the cell.
The oxygen molecules will diffuse across the membrane. The membrane of the cell is partially permeable to allow diffusion to take place.

Exercise 2.5 Describing and explaining osmosis

1   In general, the graph shows the change in *the potato's mass over time.* Specifically, it can be observed that after *2 minutes, the mass of the potato started to decrease. It decreased from 3.6 g to 2.5 g in 10 minutes.*

2   *For example*:
The mass of the potato changed because the concentration of water inside the potato was higher than the concentration of water in the salt solution. This caused water to move from the higher concentration to the lower concentration through the partially permeable membrane of the potato cells by osmosis.

3   The chemicals of life

Exercise 3.1 Chemicals of life – vocabulary

1   A/substance/that/cannot/be/broken/down/into/anything/simpler.   element

2   A/single/particle/of/an/element.   atom

3   Two/or/more/atoms/joined/together.   molecule

4   Chemical/reactions/that/take/place/in/the/body.   metabolism

5   A/useful/substance/that/makes/up/80%/of/the/body.   water

6   Molecule/that/contains/carbon/hydrogen/and/oxygen.   carbohydrate

Exercise 3.2 Sentences about carbohydrates

1   a

Prefix/Meaning	Type of sugar	Example
mono/one	*monosaccharide*	*glucose*
di-/two	disaccharide	sucrose and *maltose*
poly-/many	*polysaccharide*	cellulose and *starch*

b   polysaccharides; many

2 simple; carbon; Twelve; oxygen

3 simple; monosaccharide; plants, blood; energy

Exercise 3.3 Planning a food test

1 **a** E–1; A–2; C–3; B–4; H–5; G–6; F–7; D–8
   b A <u>Cut</u> the food up into very small pieces.
      B <u>Add</u> Benedict's solution to the test tube.
      C <u>Dissolve</u> the food in water in a test tube.
      D <u>Record</u> the results in the results chart.
      E <u>Collect</u> the necessary equipment, including your safety spectacles.
      F <u>Draw</u> a results chart.
      G <u>Observe</u> whether the solution turns orange-red showing glucose is present.
      H Strongly <u>heat</u> the test tube in a water bath.

2 **a** The food was cut up into very small pieces.
   b The food was dissolved in water in a test tube.
   c Benedict's solution was added to the test tube.
   d The test tube was strongly heated in a water bath.
   e The solution was observed to see if the colour became orange/red showing glucose was present.
   f A results chart was drawn.
   g The results were recorded in the results chart.

3 **a** **i** glucose *is the answer you are most likely to know*
         Other simple sugars you may have heard of are: fructose *and* galactose.

      ii Benedict's solution; test tubes
      iii being heated
      iv Your answer should suggest that the solution in one of the test tubes has remained a blue colour and does not contain simple sugars. You should also describe the solution in the other test tube as being *orange-red* or *brick-red*. This shows that there were simple sugars present in the food sample.
      v blue; orange-red.
   b **i** Step 1 shows two test tubes. One of the test tubes contains a solution containing protein but the other does not. There is also a bottle of Biuret' reagent, which is used to test for the presence of protein.
      ii Step 2 shows Biuret' reagent being added to the two test tubes.
      iii Step 3 shows that the solution in one of the test tubes has remained a blue colour, while the other has turned to a mauve/ purple colour.

      iv protein; Biuret' reagent; blue; mauve/ purple

Exercise 3.4 Key words for enzymes

1 catalysts; speed up; substrate; complementary; active; product; catalysing; temperature; optimum; denatured

Exercise 3.5 Effect of temperature on enzymes

1 The optimum temperature is 40 °C.

2 The enzyme begins to denature at 40 °C.

3 The enzyme is completely denatured at 56 °C.

4 The rate of reaction decreases because the enzyme is denatured and not able to carry out reactions.

5 The molecules have more kinetic energy when they are heated and heat energy is transferred to them.

Exercise 3.6 Using enzymes in industry

1 catalase; protease; lipase; isomerase; pectinase

2 **a** hydrogen peroxide
   b oxygen and water

3 fatty acids and glycerol

4 The enzymes might be denatured by higher temperatures used when washing some clothes. This causes them to lose their shape and not bind to the substrates available.

4 Animal nutrition

Exercise 4.1 Food versus nutrients

1 carbohydrates; water; proteins; fats; minerals; vitamins; fibre

2 **a** carbohydrates
   b vitamins; minerals; fibre
   c proteins
   d fats; sugars
   e water; water

Exercise 4.2 Using the correct word to suggest a more balanced diet

fewer; increase; decrease; more; decrease; smaller; more; fewer

Exercise 4.3 Carbohydrates, proteins and fats

1 carbohydrates; fats; proteins; fatty acids; amino acids; glycerol; lipase; protease; carbohydrase; glucose

2

Nutrient	Digestive enzyme	Product
carbohydrates	*carbohydrase*	simple sugars
fats/lipids	*lipase*	fatty acids and glycerol
proteins	*protease*	amino acids

3 **a** Fats/lipids are broken down by lipase to produce fatty acids and glycerol.

    b Proteins are broken down by protease into amino acids.
These answers follow the same pattern as the example given in the question.

Exercise 4.4 Digestion key words

1 Ingestion

2 Digestion

3 absorbed

4 assimilated

5 egested

6 contract

7 Deamination

Exercise 4.5 The journey of digestion

1 **a** mouth
    b oesophagus
    c stomach
    d small intestine

    e large intestine
    f rectum
    g anus
    h pancreas
    i liver

2 *Answer should include many of the following points in the story:*

  – organs listed in order: mouth; oesophagus; stomach; small intestine; pancreas; liver/gall bladder; large intestine; rectum; anus

  – enzymes: amylase breaks down starch into simple sugars; lipase breaks down lipids/fats into fatty acids and glycerol; protease breaks down proteins into amino acids

  – role of the pancreas: secretes enzymes

  – role of the liver: gall bladder secretes bile which emulsifies and neutralizes the acidic juices (chime) released from the stomach into the small intestine.

5 Plant nutrition

Exercise 5.1 Inorganic to organic

1 Organic; Inorganic

2

Organic substances	Inorganic substances
carbohydrates	*carbon dioxide*
glucose	*magnesium*
proteins	*oxygen*
starch	*water*

Exercise 5.2 Photosynthesis – word and chemical equations

1 **a** carbon dioxide + *water* $\xrightarrow[\text{chlorophyll}]{\text{sunlight}}$ *glucose* + oxygen

    $CO_2 + H_2O \xrightarrow[\text{chlorophyll}]{\text{sunlight}} C_6H_{12}O_6 + O_2$

    b Reactants; Conditions; Products

2 **a** glucose and oxygen
    b carbon dioxide and water
    c sunlight and chlorophyll

3 water; sunlight; reactants; products; photosynthesised; enters; exits/leaves; soil; organic; growth

Exercise 5.3 Limiting factors

1 less steep
decreasing

2 horizontal
constant

3 *any answer between* 0.05% *and* 0.07% *is acceptable*

4 carbon dioxide

Exercise 5.4 Leaf structure

1 **a** This is a layer of cells near the top of a leaf that contain many chloroplasts.
b These are small holes at the bottom of a leaf that allow gases to diffuse in and out.
c This prevents water escaping from the leaf through evaporation.
d This contains chlorophyll that absorbs sunlight for photosynthesis.
e These contain xylem and phloem vessels for transporting substances.
f These open and close to allow gases in and out of the stoma.

2 **a** palisade layer
b stoma
c air space
d waxy cuticle

Exercise 5.5 Mineral deficiencies

1 has yellow leaves and dead leaves (or has dead leaves and yellow leaves)
nitrates

2 has yellow leaves with dead spots
it is deficient in potassium

3 Plant D has yellow lower leaves.
Therefore, it is deficient in magnesium.

Exercise 5.6 Words to describe plants

1 **a** vessel
b absorb
c release
d simple
e transport
f guard
g factory
h limiting

2 *Your answers should*
 – *explain what the key word means*
 – *be followed by an example of a sentence using the word in a biological context.*
Good examples are given below.

a To guard means to protect and control something, such as a building. Guard cells in the stoma control how much carbon dioxide is allowed to enter the leaf.
b A vessel is a hollow container. A plant has hollow xylem vessels that transport water and minerals up the stem.
c To absorb means to take in or soak up something. The roots absorb water from the soil.
d When something is released, it is allowed to escape from where it is being held. Some of the oxygen produced by photosynthesis is released by the leaf through the stomata.
e Transport means to move something from one place to another. Water, minerals and sugars are transported around the plant to where they need to be.
f When something cannot increase, it has reached its limit. There is a limit to how much photosynthesis can happen at any one time.
g Simple means to be uncomplicated. Glucose is a simple sugar as it cannot be broken down into smaller sugars.

6 Transport in animals and plants

Exercise 6.1 Oxygen in the blood

1 **a** lungs
b body
c oxygen
d circulatory system
e heart

2 **a** to lungs
b to body
c from lungs
d left atrium
e right ventricle

Exercise 6.2 Taking care of your heart

1   **a**   smoking
    b   obesity
    c   diet
    d   stress
    e   genetics

2   **a**   avoid smoking
    b   make some changes to

3   exercises

Exercise 6.3 Blood vessels

1   **a**   thick
    b   smooth
    c   very small
    d   thin
    e   lumen
    f   muscles

2   away; towards *or* to; into; to; out; away; towards *or* to

Exercise 6.4 Effect of exercise on heart rate

1   **a**   describe
    b   describe
    c   explain
    d   explain
    e   describe
    f   describe
    g   explain
    h   describe

2   *An example of a sensible sentence would be:*
    The heart rate is increasing from 72 beats per minute to 96 beats per minute because the heart is beginning to pump blood faster around the body.
    This matches description f with explanation c. Other descriptions and explanations you can match are a–d and g–h.

Exercise 6.5 Transport in plants

1   bundle; lignin; mineral; nutrients; one direction; phloem; sieve; vascular; vessel; water; xylem

2

Xylem	Phloem	Both vessels
one direction	*nutrients*	*vascular*
water	*sieve*	*bundle*
lignin		*mineral*

3   *Your answers to these questions should use two or more sentences to describe the key word. The answer should include a description of the structure and link this to how it helps that vessel to function properly.*

   An example such as:
   a   The xylem is a hollow vessel made up of dead cells. This allows water to be transported in one direction towards the leaves where it is needed. Xylem vessels contain lignin which is strong and helps to keep the stem upright.
   b   The phloem is made up of living cells and contains sieve plates. This allows some nutrients to pass through towards the many parts of the plant where they are needed.

7 Respiration

Exercise 7.1 Equations of respiration

1   glucose; oxygen

2   carbon dioxide; water

3   energy

4   glucose + oxygen → carbon dioxide + water + energy

Exercise 7.2 Why we need respiration

1

Verb	Noun	Past participle / Adjective
contract	contraction	contracted
link	linking	linked
divide	*division*	divided
concentrate	concentration	*concentrated*
transmit	transmission	transmitted
produce	production	produced

2
  a produced
  b division
  c contraction
  d concentration
  e linked
  f transmission

3   division; contraction; concentration; transmission

Exercise 7.3 Aerobic and anaerobic respiration

1

Similarities	Differences
Both use glucose as a reactant.	Aerobic respiration produces carbon dioxide and water, whereas anaerobic respiration produces lactic acid.
Both release energy.	*Aerobic respiration releases large amounts of energy, whereas anaerobic respiration releases small amounts of energy.*
Both break down food substances to release the energy.	*Aerobic respiration requires oxygen as a reactant, while anaerobic respiration does not require oxygen.*

Exercise 7.4 Gas exchange in humans

1
  a Oxygen is passed towards the lungs down the trachea.
  b The bronchus divides into bronchioles as it enters the lungs.
  c Gas exchange takes place at the alveoli.

2

Singular term	Plural term
lung	lungs
bronchiole	*bronchioles*
bronchus	*bronchi*
alveolus	*alveoli*

Exercise 7.5 Breathing in and breathing out

1   contract; downwards; contract; upwards; increases; into

2

Part of the breathing system	What happens to this part
diaphragm	relaxes
external intercostal muscles	*relax*
rib cage	*drops down*
thorax volume	*decreases*
pressure in the lungs compared to outside the body	*higher*

3   *Answer should be a paragraph similar to the following, using the key words from the table in each sentence.*

The muscles of the diaphragm relax, which pulls the diaphragm upwards. The external intercostal muscles relax to pull the rib cage downwards. This decreases the volume of the thorax and air rushes out of the lungs. The air rushes out because the pressure in the lungs is higher than that outside the body.

8 Coordination and homeostasis

Exercise 8.1 Responding to stimuli

1   *You should have underlined the following words:* hearing; touches; eyes; hears; eyes; smell; see; smell; taste; tasting,

2   nose; ear; eye; tongue; skin

3

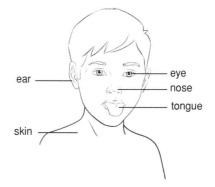

4

Sensory organ	Stimuli detected
eye	vision, light
ear	hearing, balance
nose	smell, chemical
tongue	taste, chemical
skin	touch, pain, temperature

Exercise 8.2 Reflex arcs

1 *From left to right:* sensory neurone; motor neurone; relay neurone

2 **a** The electrical ~~reaction~~ is carried to the central nervous system by a sensory neurone.
The electrical impulse is carried to the central nervous system by a sensory neurone.

b The electrical impulse is carried by a ~~sensory~~ neurone across the spinal cord.
The electrical impulse is carried by a relay neurone across the spinal cord.

c The electrical impulse is then carried away from the central nervous system along a ~~relay~~ neurone.
The electrical impulse is then carried away from the central nervous system along a motor neurone.

d The motor neurone carries the ~~chemical~~ impulse to an effector.
The motor neurone carries the electrical impulse to an effector.

e An ~~organ~~ is a muscle or gland that carries out the response to the stimulus.
An effector is a muscle or gland that carries out the response to the stimulus.

f A reflex action is ~~a voluntary~~ response to a stimulus.
A reflex action is an involuntary response to a stimulus.

g The plural of stimulus is ~~stimuluses~~.
The plural of stimulus is stimuli.

3

Reflex action	Stimulus	Response	Survival value
swallowing	*food makes contact with trachea*	*muscle above trachea contracts*	*food cannot enter trachea*

Exercise 8.3 Nervous system versus endocrine system

1 glands; hormones; thyroxine; adrenal; heart; males; testosterone; aggression

2

Feature	Nervous system	Endocrine system
made up of	*neurones*	*secretory cells*
information transmitted by	*electrical impulses*	*hormones*
messenger sent along	*nerve fibres*	blood vessels
speed at which impulse travels	*quickly*	*slowly*
length of time the effect lasts for	short amount of time	*longer amount of time*

3 In the nervous system, the impulse travels quickly but in the endocrine system it travels slowly.

4 **a** The nervous system is made up of neurones, while the endocrine system is made up of secretory cells.

b In the endocrine system, information is transmitted by hormones, whereas in the nervous system it is transmitted by electrical impulses.

c In the nervous system, the message is sent along nerve fibres, while in the endocrine system the message is sent along blood vessels.

d In the endocrine system, the effect lasts for a short amount of time but in the nervous system it lasts for a longer amount of time.

Exercise 8.4 Homeostasis

1 **a** rapid
b increases
c erect
d narrower
e less

2 **a** Hair becomes erect, which traps an insulating layer of air at the skin surface.

b Capillaries near to the surface of the skin become narrower, which reduces the amount of heat lost.

c Sweat glands produce less sweat, which prevents evaporation.

Exercise 8.5 The human excretory system

1

Statement	Number on diagram	Name of organ(s)
Carbon dioxide produced during respiration is excreted here.	1	*lungs*
Bile pigments produced here are excreted in faeces.	4	*liver*
Urea (broken-down proteins) excreted by this organ is passed out in the urine.	3	*kidneys*
Excess water and salts are removed by this organ.	2	*kidneys*

2　**a**　The liver produces bile pigments, which are excreted in the faeces.

　　b　The kidneys excrete urea, which is passed out in the urine.

　　c　The kidneys remove excess water and salts.

9　Reproduction

Exercise 9.1 Asexual and sexual reproduction

1

Feature	Asexual reproduction	Sexual reproduction
number of parents	*one*	two
are gametes present?	*no*	yes (sperm and ovum)
offspring	genetically identical	*genetically different*

2　**a**　Asexual reproduction only requires one parent whereas sexual reproduction requires two parents.

　　b　Asexual reproduction does not involve gametes, whereas sexual reproduction requires two gametes.

　　c　Asexual reproduction produces genetically identical offspring, whereas sexual reproduction produces genetically different offspring.

Exercise 9.2 The human sex cells

1

Feature of sex cell	Sperm or ovum?	Function in sex cell
nucleus	both	contains the genetic information in the chromosomes
tail	*sperm*	allows the cell to swim strongly towards the ovum
head	*sperm*	is streamlined to reduce resistance when travelling
membrane	*ovum*	prevents too many sperm penetrating the egg at one time
middle piece/body	*sperm*	contains many mitochondria to power the tail

2

Key word	Meaning
ovum	female sex cell
sperm	male sex cell
fertilise	the fusion of a sperm and an ovum
oviduct	tube that travels from the ovaries to the uterus
ovaries	the place where the ovum matures before release
ciliated	cells that contain small hairs to sweep the ovum along
ovulation	the monthly release of an ovum into the oviduct
peristalsis	the contraction and relaxation of muscles to move the ovum along the oviduct

3　ovaries; oviduct

Exercise 9.3 Puberty in males and females

1　*The following should be underlined:*
female – breasts; hair; armpits; hips; vagina; ovaries
male – chest; muscles; voice; hair; testes; sperm; penis; testosterone
The following nouns should be added:
a nipples; **b** oestrogen; **c** hair; **d** armpits; **e** testes

2 **a** oestrogen; ovaries
   b produce testosterone in the testes

3

Women	Men
breasts/nipples/vagina become larger	*develop broader chests*
hips become wider	*penis becomes larger*
armpit hair/pubic hair develops	*facial hair/armpit hair/pubic hair develops*

4

Women	Men
Become more maternal	*Become more aggressive and territorial*

5 **a** larger breasts/larger vagina/wider hips; becoming more maternal
   b men causes physical changes like broader chest, facial hair, armpit hair, pubic hair and larger penis. It also produces behavioural changes like becoming more aggressive and territorial.

Exercise 9.4 Fertilisation and implantation

1 release; reach; fuse; divides; forms; moves; sink; forms; supports

Exercise 9.5 Sexual reproduction in plants

1

Part of the plant	Function
stigma	platform for pollen to land on
stamen	the male part of the flower that is made up of the anther and the filament
petal	brightly coloured and scented to attract insects
sepal	green part of the plant and protects the flower
style	main stalk that holds the stigma in place
ovary	hollow chamber from which the ovules develop

ovule	female gamete found inside the ovary
anther	contains pollen grains and located at the end of the filament
filament	long stalk that holds the anther in place

2 *Your answer should contain sentences similar to the ones below. You should have used appropriate linking words to make your sentences flow from one to another.*

First, the pollen that is released from an anther lands on the stigma and pollination occurs. We know that the male and female gametes are haploid, which means that they contain half the number of chromosomes. Next, a pollen tube is formed down the style, which delivers the male gamete to the female gamete in the ovule. After this, the pollen tube finds a gap in the micropyle at the bottom of the style. As a result of this, fertilisation happens as the male and female gametes are able to fuse together. Finally, the zygote develops into an embryo and then a seed.

10 Inheritance and evolution

Exercise 10.1 Structure of a chromosome

1 chromatid; chromosome; gene; DNA; allele; genotype; phenotype; homologous; centromere

2 string; genetic; unit; middle; characteristics

3 specific

4 different

5 you can see it

6 *Any sensible answer such as:* eye colour; hair colour; presence of freckles; ear lobe length; hair type

7 allele

8 *From top to bottom:* homologous chromosome; centromere; chromatids

Exercise 10.2 Mitosis and meiosis

1 **a** four
   b they split
   c daughter
   d copied/replicated
   e two

2
  a two
  b two
  c they separate
  d the daughter cells
  e four

Exercise 10.3 Dominant and recessive alleles

1 brown; blue; blue

2 **a** the same
  b different
  c they have two different alleles for the same gene

3 **a** heterozygous
  b homozygous
  c heterozygous
  d heterozygous
  e homozygous
  f heterozygous

4 **a** blue eyes
  b Melissa is homozygous for blue eyes.
  c brown eyes
  d The daughter has brown eyes so must have at least one allele for brown otherwise she would have blue eyes.

5 50%

6 heterozygous

7 and **8**

		mother	
		B	b
father	B	**BB**	**Bb**
	b	**Bb**	**bb**

9 The offspring have a 75% chance of having black hair.

Exercise 10.4 Codominance and blood groups

1 **a** A and B
  b and **c**

Alleles	Phenotype
AA or Ao	Blood group A
BB or Bo	Blood group B
oo	Blood group o
AB	Blood group AB

2

		mother	
		B	o
father	A	**AB**	**Ao**
	A	**AB**	**Ao**

Your sentence should be similar to this:

The offspring have a 50% chance of having the AB blood group. This is because the alleles for blood groups A and B are codominant. This creates a third phenotype, which is blood group AB.

Exercise 10.5 Darwin and evolution

1

Key word/term	Definition
theory	a system of ideas and principles used to explain something
adapts	adjusts to new conditions
characteristic	a particular feature of a thing or an organism
variation	*having a range of different features and characteristics*
environment	*the conditions in which a species may live*

2 **a** pale (peppered) moth
  b Because they were not able to camouflage themselves against the darker trees, they were too visible to predators.
  c pollution from the nearby factory

3 a *For example:* big/strong teeth; strong legs/ strong muscles; camouflaged colour; sensitive whiskers; loud roar

b *Your answer should use sentences that link an observation to an explanation. A sample answer is provided below:*
The lion is well adapted to its environment as it has many features that allow it to hunt prey efficiently. The lion has strong muscles in its legs so that it can catch prey easily. The lion can rip and tear prey easily because it has big, strong teeth. The lion is able to camouflage itself from other animals with its golden fur. Lions also have whiskers for detecting and sensing what is around them. Finally, the lion has a very loud roar to let other animals know that they are there.

c *Your answer should describe how the population of the lions might decrease because they cannot catch as many prey. Your answer should also link this to the specific features.*
The population of the lions would decrease. They would not be able to catch as many prey if they did not have big, strong legs for running fast.

11 Ecology

Exercise 11.1 Ecological key words

1 environment; ecology; habitat; population; community; ecosystem; energy; food chain; food web

2

Word	Definition
habitat	the area where an organism lives
population	the number of organisms of the same species living together in the same area at the same time
food web	a network of food chains connected together to show the flow of energy in that ecosystem
food chain	shows the flow of energy from one organism to the next
ecology	the study of organisms and their environment
community	all of the organisms of different species that occupy the same habitat
energy	this is required for organisms to grow healthily
ecosystem	an area that contains all of the organisms and their environment
environment	the surroundings of an organism

Exercise 11.2 Food chains and food webs

1 *The boxes should be labelled in the following order from left to right:* plants are the producer; grasshopper is the primary consumer; flycatcher is the secondary consumer

2 plant; Sun; primary; grasshopper; consumer

3 a 1 producer
b 4 primary consumers
c caterpillar; grasshopper; iguana; squirrel
d secondary

4 a increase
b would increase
c If the population; population; would increase
d If the population of iguanas decreases, then the population of squirrels will increase.
Or If the population of iguanas increases, then the population of squirrels will decrease.

Exercise 11.3 The human population

1 a the population is increasing at a faster rate
b the population is increasing exponentially (or at a very fast rate)

2 *Any three sensible statements from the paragraph, such as:*
The human population has increased to over 7 billion people in recent years and most of this growth has taken place during the past 200– 300 years.
People have been getting *immunised* – which protects against disease – and so fewer people die from diseases that would have killed years before. The diets of people have also improved and this is contributing to people living much longer.

3 fossil; increase; increased; species

Exercise 11.4 Global warming and acid rain

1

Causes of acid rain	Effects of acid rain
sulfur oxides	increase soil acidity
nitrogen oxides	*wash vital minerals from soil*
combustion of fossil fuels	*plants die or have poor growth*
oxides dissolve in clouds	*lakes and rivers poisoned by washed-out minerals*

2 *Any sensible sentences that use the second conditional (If . . . would . . .):*

If we cut down fewer forests and trees, they would take in more of the carbon dioxide from the atmosphere.

If we replanted forests, they would stop water evaporating from fertile areas.

Language file

1 Types of word

1.1 Verbs

Verb forms

All verbs have three basic forms:

1. the base form
2. the past form
3. the past participle form.

Many verbs are 'regular' and so forms 2 and 3 end in '-ed'.

For example: heat, heated, heated

There are also many irregular verbs.

For example: rise, rose, risen

We just have to learn these irregular verbs.

1. The base form
   The base form of a verb has three main uses. We use this form in the present simple tense. We use this tense to talk about things which are true. For example, 'I like biology'. If we use the subjects he/she/it in the present simple, we must add 's'. For example, 'She likes biology'.

   We can also use the base form as an infinitive or imperative – see sections below for more information.

2. The past form
   We can use the past form of the verb to talk about activities that started and finished in the past. We often say when the activity happened. For example, 'Louis Pasteur discovered the principles of vaccination and pasteurisation in the 19th century.'

3. The past participle form
   The past participle form is used in science mostly when we want to make an active sentence passive. Go to Section 3.1 for more information about this.

Imperatives

Imperatives are verbs used to give instructions, orders or commands. They are used in the base or infinitive form.

For example: *Measure* the amount of carbon dioxide produced.

Evaluate how well you did the experiment.

Calculate your body mass index.

Command verbs

In tests and exams, you are given instructions as to what you should do. Below are the most common command verbs used in exams. Make sure you know what each word means, as it will help you to answer questions correctly.

Calculate	Perform a mathematical operation to find a numerical answer. You will usually need to show your working.
Comment	Give your own view on something, or evaluate data.

Compare	Say what is the same and what is different about two or more things.
Complete	Label a diagram or fill in gaps in a text or table.
Define	Give a precise description of the meaning of a term. Do not add any explanations.
Describe	Say what you can see in a graph, diagram or table *or* give the steps of what happens in a process. You do not need to give any explanation.
Discuss	Give two or more sides of an argument.
Draw	Provide a diagram, graph, etc.
Estimate	State about how much or how many. This might involve a calculation using approximate values.
Explain	You need to give reasons in your answer. Often you will need to explain why something happens, or why a process is used.
Find	Calculate, measure or otherwise determine the answer.
Interpret	Use data to draw conclusions.
List	Give a number of (usually short) points. Often the number of points required is stated in the question.
Measure	Use a measuring instrument (e.g. a ruler, callipers) to find a quantity.
Name/label	Add names or labels to a diagram.
Outline	Give the main points of a topic or process as briefly as you can.
Predict	Say what you think will happen, based on the information in the question.
Prove	Give the evidence of how you reached an answer.
Rank	Put a list of items in order, for example, of reactivity.
Refer to	Use information given as part of the question in your answer.
Show that	Give the steps of how you reached an answer.
Sketch	Provide a rough drawing, not a precise one.
Solve	Find the answer.
State	Give a short answer with no explanation, usually just simple facts. Sometimes you will be able to take the answer directly from the question.
Suggest	This could mean you need to give some of your own ideas, or to give one possible answer when there is more than one correct answer.
Support	Provide evidence/data/quotes/sources which agree with a claim or statement.

1.2 Articles

Using 'a' or 'an'

The form of 'a' or 'an' depends on the word (noun or adjective) that follows it.

If the next word begins with a consonant, use 'a':   *A* digital meter displays a numerical value.

If the next word begins with a vowel (a, e, i, o, u), use 'an':   *An* analogue meter has a scale.

You use 'a' or 'an' when you are talking about something that has not been mentioned yet, or if you are not talking about a specific thing. Once you have decided which specific thing you are talking about, you use the article 'the'.

For example: Observe an insect in the field. (This could be any insect.) Now, record the behaviour of the insect. (This is specifically the insect that you have observed.)

1.3 Adjectives

Comparatives and superlatives

We use the *comparative* to compare two things, or nouns.

We use the *superlative* when comparing three or more things.

To decide which form of the comparative and superlative to use, look at the number of syllables.

(A syllable is the number of sounds in a word. So 'atom' has two syllables: 'a'-'tom'. 'Atomic' has three: 'a'-'tom'-'ic'.)

Words of one syllable use the pattern '-er, -est' for the comparative and superlative.

For example, with 'fast':   The red car is *faster* than the blue one. The green car is the *fastest*.

Words ending in -y also use the pattern '-ier, -iest'.

For example, with 'heavy':   The wooden ball is *heavier* than the plastic ball. The steel ball is the *heaviest* ball.

Other words of two or more syllables use the patterns 'more . . . (than)', '(the) most . . .'.

For example, with 'penetrating':   Beta radiation is *more penetrating than* alpha radiation.

Gamma radiation is *the most penetrating* form of radiation.

You can use 'less . . . than' and 'the least . . .' in the same way as 'more . . . than' and 'the most . . .' to mean the opposite.

For example: Beta radiation is *less penetrating than* gamma radiation.

Alpha radiation is *the least penetrating* form of radiation.

1.4 Prepositions

Prepositions are important when constructing sentences. Prepositions are words such as 'in', 'on', 'behind', 'for', 'at' and so on. A preposition sits before a noun to show the noun's relationship to another word in the sentence. In science we often use relationships of place and time in order to talk about the position and movement of things.

Relationships of place

The car stopped *at* the supermarket.

Put the Bunsen burner *on* a heatproof mat.

The pebble was immersed *in* the water.

Relationships of time

The Hubble space telescope was launched *in* 1990.

At noon, the experiment began.

The sun sets *in* the evening.

Other uses

There are many other uses of prepositions. However, there are not really any rules for them and they often do not translate easily from language to language. Therefore we just have to learn them.

Common examples from biology include:

> We measure the length of cells *in* micrometres.

> In red blood cells, oxygen molecules bind *with* hemoglobin.

> Genes can be switched *on*.

There are many more and you should build up a list of them in your notebooks.

2 Changing words

2.1 Adding an 's'

The letter 's' is very important in the English language as it has several functions.

It's and its

It is important to understand the difference between 'it's' and 'its'. 'It's' means 'it is' while 'its' is a possessive.

For example: A liquid-in-glass thermometer is made from glass tubing. *Its* function is to measure temperature. ('Its' here means 'the function of the thermometer'.)

> Platinum is a very dense metal. *It's* denser than gold and silver. (Here 'it's' means 'it is'.)

In formal writing, as you should use in science, it is better to write 'it is' than 'it's'.

Possessives

Most possessive forms are constructed like this:

> noun + apostrophe + 's'

For example:

> *Einstein's* theory of relativity.

Note that the possessive 'its' (see above) does *not* have an apostrophe.

Plurals

Most plurals are formed by adding an 's' or 'es' to the word.

For example: A hydrogen atom has one proton while a helium atom has two protons.

There are many exceptions to this, however, especially with scientific terms: nucleus/nuclei, bacterium/bacteria, stoma/stomata. There are few rules to help with these and so they just need to be learnt.

2.2 Prefixes

There are many scientific terms that can be understood if you know the meanings of some basic prefixes, roots and suffixes. The prefix is the first part of the word, the root comes next and may be followed by a suffix.

For example, 'hypoglycemic' can be broken down into: hypo – low/below

> glyco – sugar (glucose)

> ic – pertaining to/about

So it means someone who has low blood sugar, leaving them feeling weak.

Here are some examples of prefixes and their meanings. You can find plenty of websites to help you with these:

Prefix	Meaning of the prefix	Example word	Meaning of the word
a	not, without	anaemic	without enough red blood cells
anti	against	antibiotic	against (harmful) life
ex	out	exhale	breathe out
hypo	under	hypodermic	under the skin – a hypodermic needle
in	not	inaccurate	not accurate
infra	below	infrared	below the spectrum of light rays we can see
post	after	postnatal	after giving birth

3 Types of sentence

3.1 Passive sentences

We use passive sentences when what is being done in the sentence is more important than who is doing it. The passive form focuses on the action, rather than who is performing the action. In science, the passive voice is often used in statements of fact, in describing processes and in describing experiments.

For example: Mass is measured in kilograms.

Energy is released in nuclear reactions.

The insect was attracted to the bright petals.

An active sentence follows the structure: subject + verb + (*usually*) object:

Mendel's laws describe the inheritance of biological features.

In this sentence, the subject is *Mendel's laws*.

The verb is *describe*.

The object is *the inheritance of biological features*.

To make the sentence passive, we follow some simple steps:

1. We start the sentence with the *object* of the sentence. *This object becomes the new subject.*

2. We choose a form of the verb 'to be'. The form of the verb you choose should match the tense of the verb in the active sentence. '*Describe*' is in the present tense and so we need the present form of the verb to be, i.e. *is* or *are*. '*Is*' is for singular objects and '*are*' is for plural objects.

3. We use the original verb but in its third form – the past participle form.

4. We decide if we need the original subject in our sentence or not. If we choose to keep it, then we must use the word 'by' to connect it to the sentence.

Our passive sentence, then, is:

The inheritance of biological features is described by Mendel's laws.

How do we decide if we need the original subject? Look at this example:

People carry out experiments on animals in some countries. (active)

Experiments are carried out on animals in some countries (by people). (passive)

It makes no sense to add 'by people' as this is obvious. It is quite common in science not to include the original subject.

3.2 Conditional sentences

The most common forms of conditional sentences are sentences that begin with the word 'if'.

Zero conditional

The *zero conditional* is used for facts and truths. In science, you would also use the zero conditional to describe the conclusion of an experiment.

Formed using: *If + present simple, + present simple*

For example: *If* you *heat* ice, it *melts.*

If ice *is heated*, it *melts.*

First conditional

The *first conditional* is used for things that are true as long as the action happens. In science, the first conditional is often used for predictions.

Formed using: *If + present simple, + will + the infinitive*

For example: *If* you *burn* coal, you *will pollute* the atmosphere.

If more weights *are added*, the spring *will extend* further.

In addition to 'will', we can use other modal verbs such as 'can' and 'may' in a first conditional sentence. Using 'can' and 'may' makes the statement less certain, or less probable.

Second conditional

The *second conditional* is used for situations that are possible but unlikely. In science, you might use the second conditional in discussing how a situation or process would be different if you changed the conditions.

Formed using: *If + past simple, + would + the infinitive*

For example: *If* you *studied* more, you *would pass* the exam. (The student is unlikely to study more.)

Third conditional

The *third conditional* is used for actions that did not happen. In science, it is useful when evaluating experiments.

Formed using: *If + past perfect, would + have + a past participle.*

(The *past perfect* is made using *had + a past participle.*)

For example: *If* we *had used* a microscope instead of a magnifying glass, we *would have observed* the features of the plant in more detail.

As well as 'would', we can use other modal verbs such as 'could' and 'might'.

3.3 Relative clauses

Sentences can have more than one part, or clause. We often use *defining relative clauses* where:

- ◼ the first part of the sentence introduces a word or thing (main clause)
- ◼ the second part of the sentence gives a definition of that word or thing (defining relative clause).

The two parts of the sentence are linked by a word such as 'which', 'that', 'whose' or 'when'.

We use defining relative clauses in science to write clear definitions. When writing these definitions, it is helpful to think about these headings:

The article (a/an or the), not always needed	The word or thing being defined	The verb *is* or *are*	The category the word belongs to	Which/that /whose, etc.	The rest of the sentence

For example:

An	ammeter	is	an instrument	that	measures electric current in amps.
	Cilia	are	organelles	that	sweep mucus along.
	Photosynthesis	is	a process	where	light energy is converted to chemical energy in plants.
The	moon	is	a satellite	which	orbits the Earth.

We use *non-defining relative clauses* when we are not giving a definition of the term but are giving extra information about something or someone. A non-defining relative clause is really about punctuation. We use a comma (,) before the linking words 'which', 'when', 'that' and so on.

For example: Her heart rate increased, which caused her to faint.

3.4 Negative sentences in the present simple

The sentences in 3.3 are all in the present simple. The present simple tense uses the first form of the verb. We use it to talk about facts and routines.

> I go swimming every day.
>
> He/she/it goes swimming every day.
>
> You go swimming every day.
>
> We go swimming every day.
>
> They go swimming every day.

The sun (It) rises in the east and (it) sets in the west.

To make present simple sentences negative, we need to remember two rules:

1. With the verb 'to be', the changes are:

   am – am not   I'm not worried about the exam.

   is – isn't   It isn't an arachnid – it has six legs.

   are – aren't   They aren't vegetables. Tomatoes are a fruit.

2. With all other verbs, we can use the extra, or auxiliary, verb 'do' in the negative followed by the main verb in the infinitive form (the basic form of the verb which doesn't change):

   A deciduous tree (it) **doesn't grow** cones.

   An evergreen tree (it) **doesn't drop** all of its leaves or needles in the autumn/fall or dry season.

   They **don't like** the same soil – deciduous trees need rich soil, while coniferous trees don't (need rich soil).